Handmade
Birdhouses
and Feeders

**35 projects
to attract
birds into
your garden**

Michele McKee-Orsini

photography by Caroline Arber

CICO BOOKS
LONDON NEW YORK

This edition published in 2017 by CICO Books
An imprint of Ryland Peters & Small
341 E 116th Street, New York NY 10029
20–21 Jockey's Fields, London WC1R 4BW
www.rylandpeters.com

10 9 8 7 6 5 4 3 2 1

First published in 2013

Editor: Sarah Hoggett
Designer: Mark Latter, Blue Dragonfly Ltd
Illustrator: Stephen Dew
Photographer: Caroline Arber
Stylist: Sophie Martell

Handmade
Birdhouses
and Feeders

contents

introduction

I've had several different careers in my life—pharmacy technician, photographer, fitness instructor, would-be singer—but never could I have imagined that one day I would be the author of a book on how to make birdhouses! Looking back, however, it now seems like a natural progression.

When I met my present husband, Guido, he was in working in the construction industry; I loved the fact that he was as creative as I was, so I started working with him. Soon I was working with wood, painting abstracts on walls; we even bought a run-down house, which we transformed into a model home. I soon became aware that we were getting busier than ever working under my husband's employer. We wanted to expand, but we had no license. Being the adventurous one, I took on becoming a general contractor where I learned to build houses, fix my own house, and build small pieces of furniture.

I started building birdhouses in 2009 when the economy fell and I wasn't working on the job site as much. My interest in birdhouses began largely because of where we live, in the forest, where several species of birds come around gathering string, twigs, hair, and all sorts of things to make their nests with.

Little did I know my birdhouses were going to be a big hit! I placed a few down at our local gift shop here in beautiful Forest Falls, southern California, where they all sold within three days. Now, several years later, I have a reputation for building strong and artistic birdhouses, along with my own website (BirdhousesByMichele.etsy.com) and several followers, who come each season to buy my birdhouses.

The more birdhouses I design and make, the more I realize just how much scope there is to create not only functional birdhouses, but also decorative pieces that look great in any setting. From fairly simple, rustic-looking birdhouses decorated with twigs and driftwood that I've picked up on my walks in the forest or with scraps that I've found lying around my workshop or while gardening in my yard, to brightly painted designer-style "apartments" and novelty creations such as the church on page 102 and the ship on page 110, this book contains many of my personal favorites. They will, I hope, bring birds quite literally flocking to your garden! I've included some designs for feeders, too, so that you can put out a plentiful supply of food for your feathered friends—particularly during the harsh winter months when the birds' natural food sources may be in short supply. Most of the projects require only a few basic woodworking skills and simple, readily available tools.

As we keep building houses, apartments, and industrial buildings and tearing down trees on which birds have depended, providing places for birds to nest is becoming increasingly important. If you love watching birds as much as I do, the birdhouses in this book will also provide you with endless hours of enjoyment.

basic birdhouse

Building a basic birdhouse is not as hard as it looks. With some simple tools and imagination, you can create habitats for birds to build their nest and raise their young.

Many of the projects in this book follow this basic design. It is made from dog-ear fence board, which is raw untreated wood. I use it because of its rough appearance. It's cut to the perfect width for building birdhouses for small cavity-nesting birds; for a birdhouse for larger birds, buy a wider fence board. You may want to buy two boards, to allow extra in case of cutting errors. You can buy it from your local home-improvement store.

materials

One 6 ft x 5½ in. x ½ in. (180 x 14 x 1.2 cm) dog-ear fence panel

Waterproof glue

1-in. (25-mm) finish nails or galvanized wire nails

1¼-in. (32-mm) exterior screws

Paintable wood-filler putty

80-grit sandpaper

Basic tool kit (see page 132)

cutting list

Front and back: 9¼ x 5½ in. (23.5 x 14 cm)—cut 2

Sides: 6¼ x 5½ in. (16 x 14 cm)—cut 2 (one side is reserved for the door)

Bottom roof: 5 x 5½ in. (13 x 14 cm)—cut 2

Top roof: 5¾ x 5½ in. (14.5 x 14 cm)—cut 2

Floor: 4¼ x 5½ in. (11 x 14 cm)—cut 1

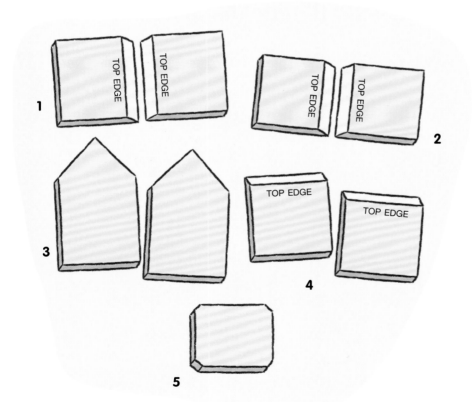

shaping the pieces

1 Bevel the top edges of the side panels at a 45° angle.

2 Bevel the top edges of the bottom roof panels at a 45° angle, then cut each in half so they measure 5 x 2¾ in. (13 x 7 cm).

3 Cut the peaks of the front and back panels at a 45° angle.

4 Bevel the top edges of the top roof panels at a 45° angle.

5 Cut approx. ¼ in. (6 mm) diagonally off all four corners of the floor panel. This is for drainage on the bottom of the box.

Constructing the birdhouse

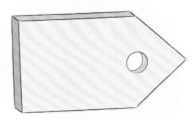

1 Place the front panel rough side down and drill the entrance hole. (See chart on pages 140–41 for the desired height and hole diameter for specific bird species.)

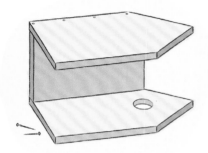

2 With the rough sides facing in, glue and nail one side panel to the inside edges of the front and back panels. Leave the other side open for the door.

3 Slide the floor panel in place between the front and back panels, without applying glue, then slide the remaining side panel (which will become the door) in place to ensure that it will fit flush with the edges of the front and back panels when the door is closed. If the door is not flush, cut the necessary amount off the floor. Glue and nail the floor panel in place.

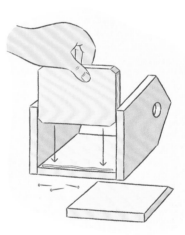

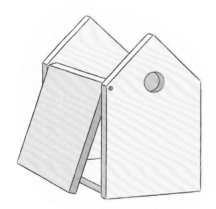

4 Place the door panel between the front and back panels. Use a speed square to line up where the pilot holes will be placed on the front and back edges: the screws need to be directly across from each other in order for the door to swing open properly. Using a ⅛-in. (3-mm) bit, drill a pilot hole through the front and back panels into the door below the point at which the roof slopes upward. Insert a 1¼-in. (32-mm) exterior screw at each point to act as hinges for the door.

5 Glue and nail the beveled edges of each pair of bottom roof panels together. Glue and nail one set of bottom roof panels in place over the front of the birdhouse, flush with the inside edge of the panel. The overhang at the front will protect the entrance hole during rainy weather.

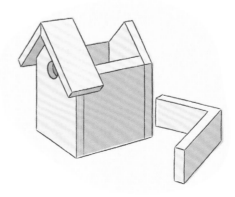

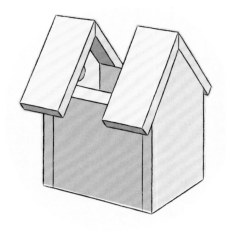

6 Glue and nail the other set of bottom roof panels flush with the outside edge of the back panel for a wall mount or overhanging the back panel by 1 in. (25 mm) if you are going to hang the birdhouse from its roof.

7 Glue and nail the top roof panels together along the beveled edges. Center the top roof on the bottom roof, which creates vent ducts. Glue and nail the top and bottom roof panels together.

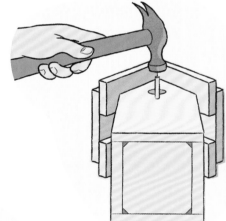

8 Fill all holes with paintable wood-filler putty, then sand the birdhouse lightly with 80-grit sandpaper to knock off any splinters and smooth the putty flush with the wood.

9 Drill a hole for the dowel perch, using a ⁵⁄₁₆-in. (3-mm) drill bit. Cut a ⁵⁄₁₆-in. (3-mm) wooden dowel rod to 1¾ in. (45 mm) in length. Hammer the dowel rod into the hole until only ¾ in. (20 mm) protrudes on the outside of the birdhouse.

10 Prepare for painting by brushing off any excess dust and placing tape or wadded paper in the hole. This keeps the inside of the hole and the interior of the birdhouse free of paint, as it is important for the birds that the inside is clean, natural wood.

simple roof

Several of the projects in this book feature this simple roof, which involves no mitering. Simply cut the roof pieces to the dimensions given in the project instructions, then follow the steps below.

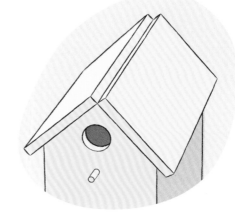

1 The project instructions will tell you whether the roof pieces should be flush with the back or front panels of the birdhouse or whether they should overhang. Glue and nail the roof pieces in place, so that they touch along the center ridge. This will leave a V-shaped gap on the roof ridge.

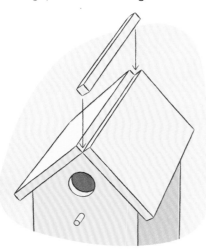

2 Cut a piece of 1 x 1-in. (2.5 x 2.5-cm) square dowel to the length required. Glue and nail it into the V-shaped gap, angling the nails slightly so that they go through both the dowel and the roof piece. (Again, the individual project instructions will tell you whether the dowel is to be positioned flush with the back/front of the birdhouse or to overhang.)

chapter 1

rustic birdhouses

In this chapter you'll find birdhouses made using natural
elements, such as bark, driftwood, moss, and wire. There
are a variety of unique combinations, from simple to classic
birdhouses, that provide ample room for birds to nest
and raise their young.

Attract small cavity-nesting birds to your garden with this rustic but simple birdhouse. A wire attached to the roof makes it easy to hang. Small pieces of driftwood are used on the front façade and for the door knob, with moss tucked in between the cracks.

simple birdhouse

materials

One 6 ft x 5½ in. x ½ in. (180 x 14 x 1.2 cm) dog-ear fence panel

Waterproof glue

1-in. (25-mm) finish nails or galvanized wire nails

2 x 1¼-in. (30-mm) exterior screws for doors

3 x 1¼-in. (30-mm) exterior screws for driftwood pieces

1¾-in. (4.5-cm) length of round dowel, ⁵⁄₁₆ in. (8 mm) in diameter, for perch

10½-in. (26.5-cm) length of 1 x 1-in. (2.5 x 2.5-cm) square dowel

26-in. (66-cm) length of heavy wire

Paintable wood-filler putty

80-grit sandpaper

Gray wood-primer paint

Yellow oil-based exterior spray paint

Dark brown exterior craft paint

Small pieces of driftwood

Moss

Water-based exterior varnish

Basic tool kit (see page 132)

finished size

Approx. 10½ x 6½ x 5½ in. (26.5 x 16.5 x 14 cm)

interior dimensions

Floor area: 4¼ x 5½ in. (10.75 x 14 cm)

Cavity depth: 8 in. (20 cm)

Entrance hole to floor: 6 in. (15 cm)

Entrance hole: 1½ in. (40 mm) in diameter

cutting list

Front and back: 9¼ x 5½ in. (23.5 x 14 cm)—cut 2

Sides: 6½ x 5½ in. (16.5 x 14 cm)—cut 2 (one side is reserved for the door)

Roof: 8¾ x 5½ in. (22 x 14 cm)—cut 2

Floor: 4¼ x 5½ in. (11 x 14 cm)—cut 1

1 Referring to the Basic Birdhouse on pages 8–10, cut and shape the birdhouse pieces from dog-ear fence board; do not bevel the roof panels. Cut a 1½-in. (40-mm) entrance hole, 6½ in. (16.5 cm) from the bottom of the front panel and centered on the width.

2 Assemble the body of the birdhouse, following steps 2–4 of the Basic Birdhouse on page 9. Attach the roof, following the instructions for the Simple Roof on page 11, with the square dowel overlapping each end of the roof by 1 in. (2.5 cm). Using a ⁵⁄₁₆-in. (8-mm) bit, drill a hole in the front panel, 1 in. (2.5 cm) below the entrance hole, and insert a length of round dowel for the perch (see step 9 on page 10).

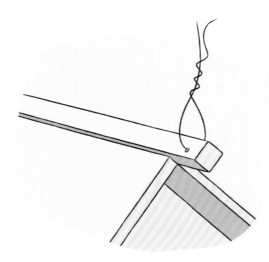

3 Drill a ⅛-in. (3-mm) hole through each overlapping end of the square dowel on the roof. Thread the end of the wire through and twist several times to secure. Make a hanging loop in the center of the wire by twisting the wire around several times.

4 Prepare the birdhouse for painting (see step 10 on page 10). Allowing the paint to dry between coats, prime the birdhouse all over (including the base) with gray paint, then paint the body of the box yellow. Lightly sand the body of the birdhouse so that some of the gray shows through. Dilute dark brown exterior paint, 1 part paint to 2 parts water, and paint the roof. Sand the edges of the birdhouse and roof to give a worn look.

5 Using a ⅛-in. (3-cm) bit, drill pilot holes for screws in the driftwood sticks for the front panel. Countersink the screw heads (see page 135), then screw in place, taking care not to overtighten. Apply a little glue and press on moss to hide the screw heads. Now apply a little glue to the side of the driftwood and tuck moss under and around the edge. Pre-drill a pilot hole through the back of the door into a small piece of driftwood for the door knob. Screw the door knob in place.

6 Plug the entrance hole with wadded-up paper or tape, then varnish the exterior of the birdhouse (see page 132).

With bark and moss attached to the roof and front, this is a very traditional-style birdhouse. Driftwood accents the front eaves and provides a unique knob for the clean-out door.

tree-bark **birdhouse**

materials

One 6 ft x 5½ in. x ½ in. (180 x 14 x 1.2 cm) dog-ear fence panel

Waterproof glue

1-in. (25-mm) finish nails or galvanized wire nails

1¼-in. (30-mm) exterior screws

1¾-in. (4,5-cm) length of round dowel, 5⁄16 in. (8 mm) in diameter, for perch

Paintable wood-filler putty

80-grit sandpaper

Sage green oil-based exterior spray paint

Pine and oak bark

Small piece of driftwood for door knob

6–8-in. (15–20-cm) driftwood stick

Loose moss

26-in. (66-cm) length of heavy wire

2 x 1¼-in. (32-mm) screw eyes

Water-based exterior varnish

Basic tool kit (see page 132)

finished size

Approx. 11 x 6¾ x 5½ in. (28 x 16 x 14 cm)

interior dimensions

Floor area: 4¼ x 5½ in. (11 x 14 cm)

Cavity depth: 8 in. (20 cm)

Entrance hole to floor: 6 in. (15 cm)

Entrance hole: 1¼ in. (32 mm) in diameter

cutting list

Front and back: 9¼ x 5½ in. (23.5 x 14 cm)—cut 2

Sides: 6¼ x 5½ in. (16 x 14 cm)—cut 2 (one side is reserved for the door)

Bottom roof: 5 x 5½ in. (13 x 14 cm)—cut 2

Top roof: 5¾ x 5½ in. (14.5 x 14 cm)—cut 2

Floor: 4¼ x 5½ in. (11 x 14 cm)—cut 1

1 Referring to the Basic Birdhouse on pages 8–10, cut and shape the birdhouse pieces from dog-ear fence board. Reserve one of the triangular pieces that you cut off the front panel. Cut a 1¼-in. (32-mm) entrance hole, 6½ in. (16.5 cm) from the bottom of the front panel, centered on the width.

2 Assemble the birdhouse, following steps 2–9 of the Basic Birdhouse on pages 9–10. Prepare the birdhouse for painting (see step 10 on page 10), then paint green and leave to dry.

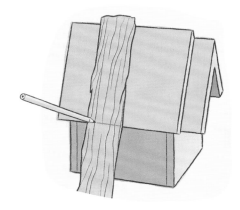

3 Place your pieces of bark on the roof and mark with a pencil where you need to cut.

4 Glue moss along the ridge of the roof, then glue each piece of bark in turn and apply, gluing small pieces of moss along the bottom edge of the roof as you go. Nail the bark top, center, and bottom so that it's securely attached. If the roof of the birdhouse shows through in places, glue in small pieces of moss to cover it.

5 Using a ⅟₁₆-in. (1.5-mm) bit, pre-drill a hole for the screw eye 1 in. (2.5 cm) below the point of the birdhouse on the front and back. Use needle-nose pliers to twist in the screw eyes securely. Attach wire to the screw eyes to hang the birdhouse.

6 Using a ⅛-in. (3-mm) bit, drill a pilot hole through the driftwood stick and the eave of the roof. Countersink the hole with a ⁵⁄₁₆-in. (8-mm) bit to hide the screw head, then carefully sink the screw in. Drill a pilot hole (see page 136) through from the back of the door and screw on the driftwood door knob.

7 Lightly sand the front of the birdhouse. Glue a piece of moss to the front, slightly off-center. Using a ⅛-in. (3-mm) bit, drill a pilot hole in the front, then screw a piece of bark in place with a ⅝-in. (1.5-cm) exterior screw. Varnish the exterior of the birdhouse (see page 132).

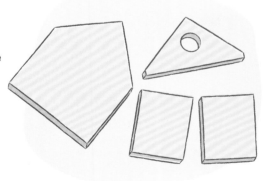

Blue Tit

With its blue body and rustic accent of driftwood pieces, rope, and shells, this birdhouse is cuteness personified. The front doors open for nest removal, while a small wire latch keeps the doors from opening while the birdhouse is in use.

blue barn **birdhouse**

materials

6 ft x 5½ in. x ½ in. (180 x 14 x 1.2 cm) dog-ear fence board

Waterproof glue

1-in. (25-mm) finish nails or galvanized wire nails

9-in. (23-cm) length of 1 x 1-in. (25 x 25-mm) square wood dowel

4 x ⅞-in. (87-mm) square distressed hinges

3 x 1¼-in. (30-mm) exterior screws

3 driftwood pieces, 2–4 in. (5–10 cm) long

Shells

Short lengths of worn rope

5-in. (12.5-cm) length of heavy black wire

Paintable wood-filler putty

80-grit sandpaper

Deep blue oil-based exterior spray paint

Dark brown exterior craft paint

2 x 2-in. (5-cm) exterior screws

Water-based exterior varnish

Basic tool kit (see page 132)

finished size

Approx. 13¼ x 5½ x 7½ in. (33.5 x 14 x 19 cm)

interior dimensions

Floor area: 4¼ x 5½ in. (10.5 x 14 cm)

Cavity depth: 5¾ in. (14.5 cm)

Entrance hole to floor: 4 in. (10 cm)

Entrance hole: 1⅛ in. (28 mm) in diameter

cutting list

Front and back: 6½ x 5½ in. (16.5 x 14 cm)—cut 2

Sides: 3¾ x 5½ in. (9.5 x 14 cm)—cut 2 (one side is reserved for the door)

Roof: 8 x 5½ in. (20 x 14 cm) — cut 2

Floor: 4¼ x 5½ in. (11 x 14 cm)—cut 1

Back mount panel: 13¾ x 5½ in. (35 x 14 cm)—cut 1

1 Referring to the Basic Birdhouse on page 8, shape the front and back panels. Cut a 1⅛-in. (28-mm) entrance hole in the front panel, positioning it 4½ in. (11.5 cm) from the bottom and centered on the panel width. Draw a straight line across the front panel at the point where the sides slope upward, and cut off the triangular-shaped top. Cut about ¼ in. (6 mm) off the left and right ends of the triangle. Cut the rest of the front panel in half lengthwise.

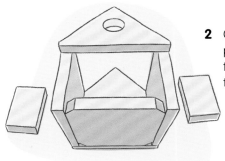

2 Glue and nail back the panel to the side panels, reserving the front panel sections for the doors. Glue and nail the front triangle piece to the top of the side panels.

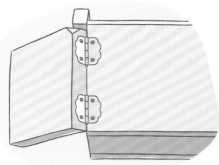

3 Cut a small piece off the upper hinge side corner of each door at a 45° angle where the roof will touch the door. Using a ⅛-in. (3-mm) bit, drill a pilot hole (see page 136) on the sides of the doors and the side panels as a starting point for the screws. Attach two small hinges to each side panel and door section. They need to lie flat, otherwise the doors will not open properly.

4 Attach the roof panels and strip of square dowel, following the instructions for the Simple Roof on page 11. Add a triangle of wood to the front, just below the eaves, to add character.

5 Attach the birdhouse to the back mount board.

6 Spraying straight onto the raw wood, paint the birdhouse and back mount panel deep blue. Leave to dry, then lightly sand with 80-grit sandpaper. Paint the roof with watered-down, dark brown, exterior craft paint. Leave to dry, then lightly sand the edges for a worn look.

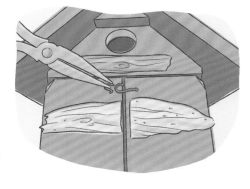

7 Nail or glue the driftwood pieces in place. Using a ⅛-in. (3-mm) bit, make a small hole on each side of the door. Thread the wire through, then twist the ends together with pliers to create a latch to close the doors. Slightly twist the wire on the back of the door so it does not pull through.

8 Using a ⁵⁄₁₆-in. (8-mm) bit, make angled ventilation holes just under the eaves. Brush off all sawdust, then varnish with water-based exterior varnish (see page 132).

With all the natural elements —moss, driftwood, and bark—this birdhouse is sure to attract a tenant. I found a single piece of bark with a perfectly centered hole, but if your piece of bark has the hole off center, that's ok—the birds won't care! Alternatively, you can drill your own hole. The front panel needs to be painted before it is attached to the sides, so that you can place the hole in the bark directly over the entrance hole.

woodland **birdhouse**

materials

One 6 ft x 5½ in. x ½ in. (180 x 14 x 1.2 cm) dog-ear fence board

Waterproof glue

1-in. (25-mm) finish nails or galvanized wire nails

Piece of bark approx. 10 in. (25 cm) in length, with 1½-in. (40-mm) hole

12 x 1¼-in. (30-mm) exterior screws

2 x ¾-in. (20-mm) wood screws

Paintable wood-filler putty

80-grit sandpaper

Brown and off-white oil-based exterior spray paints

5–7 driftwood sticks

Moss

1 x 1-in. (25-mm) EMT two-hole pipe clamp (clip)

Water-based exterior varnish

Basic tool kit (see page 132)

finished size

Approx. 14 x 6¾ x 5½ in. (35.5 x 17 x 14 cm)

interior dimensions

Floor area: 4¼ x 5½ in. (10.75 x 14 cm)

Cavity depth: 11 in. (28 cm)

Entrance hole to floor: 7 in. (18 cm)

Entrance hole: 1½ in. (4 cm) in diameter

cutting list

Front and back: 12 x 5½ in. (30 x 14 cm)—cut 2

Sides: 10 x 5½ in. (25 x 14 cm)—cut 2 (one side is reserved for the door)

Bottom roof: 5 x 5½ in. (12.5 x 14 cm)—cut 2

Top roof: 5¾ x 5½ in. (14.5 x 14 cm)—cut 2

Floor: 4¼ x 5½ in. (11 x 14 cm)—cut 1

1 Referring to the Basic Birdhouse on page 8, cut and shape the birdhouse pieces from dog-ear fence board—but before cutting the 45° peak of the front panel, place the bark on the front panel and draw a circle through the hole in the bark to mark where the entrance hole is to be cut. Then shape the front panel and cut the entrance hole.

2 Assemble the back, side panel, door panel, and base of the birdhouse, following steps 2–4 on page 9 and keeping the front panel to one side.

3 Prepare the birdhouse for painting (see step 10 on page 10), then paint the exterior of the front panel brown and leave to dry. Repeat with off-white paint and leave to dry. Lightly sand the front panel to create a worn look.

4 Using a ⅛-in. (3-mm) bit, drill pilot holes from the back of the front panel through to the front, then use 1¼-in. (30-mm) wood screws to attach the bark to the front panel.

Winter Wren

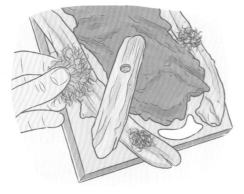

5 Glue and nail the front panel to the side panel; do not nail the side that is adjacent to the door yet.

6 Complete the birdhouse, following steps 5–10 of the Basic Birdhouse on pages 9–10.

7 Mask off the front panel, then paint the rest of the body of the birdhouse in the same colors. Paint the roof brown. Leave to dry.

8 Attach the driftwood pieces with 1¼-in. (30-mm) exterior screws. Apply a tiny amount of waterproof glue over each screw head, then cover the screw heads with moss, tucking the moss in around the driftwood where desired.

9 Remove the door panel, drill a pilot hole (see page 136) through the back of the door panel and the driftwood stick for the door pull, and then insert a 1¼-in. (30-mm) exterior screw to attach the door pull. Replace the door panel, attaching it to the front and back panels (see step 4 on page 9).

10 Attach a 1-in. (25-mm) EMT two-hole pipe clamp (clip) to the apex of the roof for a hanging loop (see page 138).

11 Plug the entrance hole with wadded-up paper or tape, then varnish the birdhouse (see page 132). Hang the birdhouse from the pipe-strap fastener.

The vibrant green color and three-tiered roof will make this birdhouse a talking point in any garden. Hanging it from a piece of driftwood is a suitably rustic-looking touch and ties in visually with the decorative elements on the front of the birdhouse.

triple-roof hanging birdhouse

materials

One 6 ft x 5½ in. x ½ in. (180 x 14 x 1.2 cm) dog-ear fence panel

Waterproof glue

1-in. (25-mm) finish nails or galvanized wire nails

1¼-in. (30-mm) exterior screws for door and driftwood

1¾-in. (4.5-cm) length of round dowel, 5⁄16 in. (8 mm) in diameter, for perch

Paintable wood-filler putty

80-grit sandpaper

Brown wood primer paint

Green oil-based exterior spray paint

5 driftwood pieces, approx. 3–7 in. (7.5–18 cm) long

1 x 1-in. (25-mm) EMT two-hole pipe clamp (clip)

2 x ¾-in. (20-mm) wood screws for pipe strap fastener

2 x 7-in. (18-cm) length of heavy wire

Exterior craft paints (optional)

Water-based exterior varnish

Basic tool kit (see page 132)

finished size

Approx. 12 x 6¾ x 5½ in. (30 x 17 x 14 cm)

interior dimensions

Floor area: 4¼ x 5½ in. (10.75 x 14 cm)

Cavity depth: 8 in. (20 cm)

Entrance hole to floor: 6 in. (15 cm)

Entrance hole: 1¼ in. (32 mm) in diameter

cutting list

Front and back: 9¼ x 5½ in. (23.5 x 14 cm)—cut 2

Sides: 6¼ x 5½ in. (16 x 14 cm)—cut 2 (one side is reserved for the door)

Bottom roof: 5 x 5½ in. (13 x 14 cm)—cut 2

Center roof: 5¾ x 5½ in. (14.5 x 14 cm)—cut 2

Third roof: 4 x 5¼ in. (10 x 13.5 cm)—cut 2

Floor: 4¼ x 5½ in. (11 x 14 cm)—cut 1

1   Referring to the Basic Birdhouse on page 8, cut and shape the birdhouse pieces from dog-ear fence board. Cut a 1¼-in. (32-mm) entrance hole, 6½ in. (16.5 cm) from the bottom of the front panel and centered on the width.

2   Assemble the birdhouse, following steps 2–8 of the Basic Birdhouse on pages 9–10, then glue and nail the third roof on top of the center roof.

3   Drill a hole and insert a length of round dowel for the perch (see step 9 on page 10).

4   Prepare the birdhouse for painting (see step 10 on page 10). Allowing the paint to dry between coats, prime the birdhouse all over (including the base) with brown paint, then paint the body of the box with green paint. Lightly sand the body of the birdhouse so that some of the brown shows through. Dilute dark brown exterior craft paint, 1 part paint to 2 parts water, and paint the roof, leaving the front trim green. Leave to dry. Sand the edges of the roof to give a worn look.

5 Attach a 1-in. (25-mm) EMT two-hole pipe clamp (clip) to the apex of the roof for a hanging loop (see page 138).

6 Take a 7-in. (18-cm) length of driftwood stick and drill a small hole at each end for the hanging wire. Thread one wire through one hole and then through the loop of the pipe clamp (clip), and twist both ends of the wire together with pliers to secure. Form another wire loop at the other end of the driftwood for hanging the birdhouse.

7 Remove the door. Using a ⅛-in. (3-mm) bit, drill pilot holes (see page 136) through from the back, then attach one driftwood piece to the door to act as a knob and others to the front for decoration, using 1¼-in. (30-mm) screws. Replace the door. If you wish, paint flowers on the front panel, using exterior craft paints.

8 Plug the entrance hole with wadded-up paper or tape, then varnish the exterior of the birdhouse (see page 132).

Traveling to the beach is a fond memory of mine, and picking up all sorts of shells and pieces of driftwood gave me the inspiration for a nautical-themed birdhouse.

seaside birdhouse

materials

Two 6 ft x 5½ in. x ½ in. (180 x 14 x 1.2 cm) dog-ear fence boards

Waterproof glue

1-in. (25-mm) finish nails or galvanized wire nails

2 x 1¼-in. (30-mm) exterior screws

2 x 2-in. (50-mm) exterior screws

Three lengths of ⁵⁄₁₆-in (8-mm) round dowel, 1, 1½, and 1¾ in. (2.5, 4 and 4.5 cm) long respectively, for perches

Three 5½ x ½-in. (14 x 1.2-cm) strips of dog-ear fence panel for ledges

18¼ x 3½ in. (46.5 x 9 cm) dog-ear fence board for back mount panel

Paintable wood-filler putty

80-grit sandpaper

Dark brown and ivory oil-based exterior spray paints

Brown exterior craft paint

Water-based exterior varnish

Seaside-themed embellishments of your choice—for example, star fish, shells, rope ½ in. (12 mm) in diameter

3 skeleton keys (optional)

Weatherproof silicone glue and glue gun and exterior glue sticks

Basic tool kit (see page 132)

finished size

Approx. 14 x 5½ x 6⅜ in. (35.5 x 14 x 16 cm)

Back panel mount: 18½ x 5½ in. (50 x 14 cm)

interior dimensions

Floor area: 4¼ x 5½ in. (11 x 14 cm)

Cavity depth: 11½ in. (29 cm)

Entrance hole to floor: 10 in. (25 cm)

Entrance hole: 1¼ in. (32 mm)

cutting list

Front and back: 12¼ x 5½ in. (31 x 14 cm)—cut 2

Sides: 9½ x 5½ in. (24 x 14 cm)—cut 2 (one side is reserved for the door)

Bottom roof: 5 x 5½ in. (20 x 14 cm) —cut 2

Top roof: 5¾ x 5½ in. (14.5 x 14 cm)—cut 2

Floor: 4¼ x 5½ in. (11 x 14 cm)—cut 1

Back panel mount: 18-½ x 5½ in. (50 x 14 cm)—cut 1 from dog-ear end of fence board

1 Referring to the Basic Birdhouse on page 8, cut and shape the birdhouse pieces from dog-ear fence board. Cut a 1¼-in. (32-mm) entrance hole, 10 in. (25 cm) from the bottom of the front panel and centered on the width. Then, assemble the birdhouse and prepare it for painting, following steps 2–8 of the Basic Birdhouse on pages 9–10.

2 Using a ⁵⁄₁₆-in. (8-mm) bit, drill three holes below the entrance hole for perches, spacing them randomly. Tap the 1-in. (2.5-cm) length of dowel into the left-hand hole, the 1½-in. (4-cm) length into the center hole, and the 1¾-in. (4.5-cm) length into the right-hand hole, leaving each one sticking out slightly further than the previous one.

3 Cut three 5½ x ½-in. (14.5 x 1.2-cm) pieces from fence panel for the front ledges. Lay the first piece across the roof from edge to edge, mark on the back, then cut at a 45° angle on each side. Glue and nail in place. Glue and nail the second piece 5 in. (13 cm) above the base of the front panel. Cut the third piece to approx. 3 in. (7.5 cm) long and at a 45° angle at one end to make the last ledge. Glue and nail it 1½ in. (4 cm) from the bottom.

4 Using a ⅛-in. (3-mm) bit, drill two pilot holes in the dog-ear end of the mount board for 2-in. (5-cm) exterior screws. Using a ⅛-in. (3-mm) bit, drill pilot holes through the back of the birdhouse, then drill in 1¼-in. (30-mm) exterior screws to attach the birdhouse to the back mount board.

5 Paint the birdhouse and back mount panel dark brown and leave to dry. Next, paint the top coat in ivory and leave to dry. Then paint the dowel perches and ledges dark brown and wipe with a rag while wet to get a translucent effect. Dilute 1 part brown exterior craft paint to 2 parts water and paint the roof to create a worn effect.

6 Using weatherproof silicone glue or a glue gun with exterior glue sticks, attach your chosen embellishments wherever you choose. If you're using rope or small keys, nail them in place for extra security.

7 Drill a hole through the door with the appropriate size of bit. Push the neck of the door knob through the hole and attach with a washer and a nut.

This birdhouse can be placed on an outdoor shelf or hung in a covered patio corner to invite the birds to nest. The muted colors and bleached driftwood embellishments make a rustic, folk art-style addition to your garden.

rustic nesting box

materials

One 6 ft x 5½ in. x ½ in. (180 x 14 x 1.2 cm) dog-ear fence board

Waterproof glue

1-in. (25-mm) finish nails or galvanized wire nails

1 x 1¾-in. (4.5-cm) length of round dowel, ⁵⁄₁₆ in. (8 mm) in diameter, for perch

3 driftwood sticks, approx. 5 in. (12.5 cm) long

2 x 1-in. (5 x 2.5-cm) piece of driftwood for door knob

1 x 1-in. (25-mm) EMT two-hole pipe clamp (clip)

2 x ¾-in. (20-mm) wood screws for pipe strap fastener

10 x 1¼-in. (30-mm) exterior screws for door and driftwood

80-grit sandpaper

Paintable wood-filler putty

White and brown wood-primer paint

Sage green oil-based exterior spray paint

Dark brown exterior craft paint

Water-based exterior varnish

Basic tool kit (see page 132)

finished size

Approx. 14 x 6¾ x 5½ in. (35.5 x 17 x 14 cm)

interior dimensions

Floor area: 4¼ x 5½ in. (10.75 x 14 cm)

Cavity depth: 10 in. (25 cm)

Entrance hole to floor: 8 in. (20 cm)

Entrance hole: 1¼ in. (32 mm) in diameter

cutting list

Front and back: 12 x 5½ in. (30 x 14 cm)—cut 2

Sides: 9 x 5½ in. (23 x 14 cm)—cut 2 (one side is reserved for the door)

Bottom roof: 5 x 5½ in. (13 x 14 cm)—cut 2

Top roof: 5¾ x 5½ in. (14.5 x 14 cm)—cut 2

Floor: 4¼ x 5½ in. (10.75 x 14 cm)—cut 1

1 Cut a strip 1 in. (25 mm) deep across the width of the dog-ear fence board for the decorative shelf on the front of the birdhouse. Referring to the Basic Birdhouse on page 8, cut the birdhouse pieces from dog-ear fence board and shape them.

2 Cut a 1¼-in. (32-mm) entrance hole in the front panel, 8½ in. (21.5 cm) from the bottom of the front panel and centered on the panel width. Drill a ⁵⁄₁₆-in. (8-mm) hole for the strip of dowel rod to be inserted halfway through. Glue, then nail the shelf to the front. Assemble the birdhouse and prepare for painting, following steps 1–10 of the Basic Birdhouse on pages 9–10.

3 Apply white primer to the exterior front, back, sides, and base, and brown primer to the roof exterior. Leave to dry. Apply sage green paint to the exterior front, back, sides, and base, and leave to dry. Lightly sand, so that some of the white primer shows through. Dilute dark brown exterior craft paint to 1 part paint and 2 parts water and paint the roof and the shelf.

4 Remove the door. Using a ⅛-in. (3-mm) bit, drill pilot holes through from the back of the front panel to the front, and attach a short and a long driftwood stick above and below the shelf, using 1¼-in. (30-mm) exterior screws. Attach the driftwood door knob in the same way. Alternatively, nail the pieces on from the front.

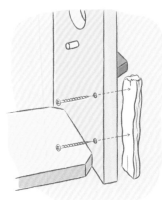

5 Now make the three wooden circles that sit on the right of the shelf from the remaining driftwood stick. Glue them together, let dry, then glue them on top of the shelf.

6 Attach a 1-in. (25-mm) EMT two-hole pipe clamp (clip) to the apex of the roof for a hanging loop (see page 138).

7 Plug the entrance hole with wadded-up paper or tape, then varnish the birdhouse (see page 132). Hang the birdhouse from the pipe strap fastener.

This delightful red farmhouse can be mounted easily on a tree, fence, or patio wall and accommodates the tufted titmouse and other small cavity-nesting birds.

red farmhouse
birdhouse

materials

One 6 ft x 5½ in. x ½ in.
  (180 x 14 x 1.2 cm) dog-ear fence panel

20-in. (50-cm) length of 1 x 1-in.
  (25 x 25-mm) square dowel

Waterproof glue

1-in. (25-mm) finish nails
  or galvanized wire nails

2 x 1¼-in. (30-mm) exterior screws

3½ x 17½ in. (9 x 44.5 cm) dog-ear
  fence panel for back mount board

3 x 2-in. (50-mm) exterior screws

1 x 1¾-in. (4.5-cm) length of round dowel,
  ⁵⁄₁₆ in. (8 mm) in diameter, for perch

Dark red oil-based exterior spray paint

White, dark brown, and green
  exterior craft paint

Water-based exterior varnish

Basic tool kit (see page 132)

finished size

Approx. 14 x 6¾ x 5½ in. (35.5 x 17 x
  14 cm)

interior dimensions

Floor area: 4¼ x 5½ in. (11 x 14 cm)

Cavity depth: 9 in. (23 cm)

Entrance hole to floor: 6 in. (15 cm)

Entrance hole: 1¼ in. (32 mm) in diameter

cutting list

Front and back: 9¼ x 5½ in.
  (23.5 x 14 cm)—cut 2

Sides: 6¼ x 5½ in. (16 x 14 cm)—cut 2
  (one side is reserved for the door)

Bottom roof: 5 x 5½ in. (13 x 14 cm)—cut 2

Top roof: 5¾ x 5½ in. (14.5 x 14 cm)—cut 2

Floor: 4¼ x 5½ in. (11 x 14 cm)—cut 1

Back mount panel: 17½ x 3½ in. (44.5 x
  9 cm)—cut 1

1 Referring to the Basic Birdhouse on page 8, cut and shape the birdhouse pieces from dog-ear fence board. Reserve one of the triangular pieces that you cut off the front panel. Cut a 1¼-in. (32-mm) entrance hole, 6½ in. (16.5 cm) from the bottom of the front panel and centered on the width.

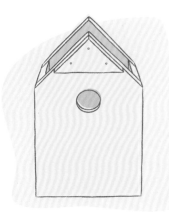

2 Assemble the walls and floor, following steps 2–4 of the Basic Birdhouse on page 9. Glue, then nail the reserved triangular piece from step 1 to the top of the front panel, with the longest edge at the base.

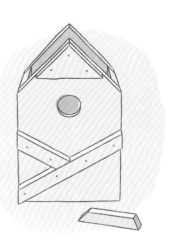

3 Place the 1 x 1-in. (25 x 25-mm) square dowel across the front panel in the desired location. Using a pencil, make a mark from the back to give you the length and the angle of cut. Cut to size, then glue and nail in place. Attach two shorter lengths diagonally across the first in the same way to form a cross. The cut on the end of the first length will be the correct angle of cut for the next two pieces.

4 Cut a 3½-in. (9-cm) length of 1 x 1-in. (25 x 25-mm) square dowel for the door knob. Using a ⅛-in. (3-mm) bit, drill a pilot hole (see page 136) from the back of the door through the door knob. Glue and nail the door knob in place, then insert a 1¼-in. (30-mm) screw from the back of the door for extra security.

5 Complete the birdhouse and prepare it for painting, following steps 5–10 of the Basic Birdhouse on pages 9–10. Attach the birdhouse to the back mount board.

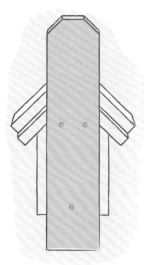

6 Paint the exterior of the birdhouse (except for the cross) and the back mount board red. Next, paint the roof brown; when it is dry, lightly brush on some green paint here and there to create a rustic, weathered look. Then paint the eaves, cross, and door knob white. Varnish the birdhouse (see page 132), then attach some moss to the front using waterproof glue.

The technique used for giving this birdhouse an old weathered look of running paint is the same as that used in the process of refinishing furniture. The left side of the birdhouse lifts up to remove an unoccupied nest. Air vents are drilled on one side to keep occupants cool in warmer weather. There is a mount from top to bottom for securing to a post or a tree.

secret hideout

materials

Two 6ft x 7½ in. x ½-in. (180 x 19 x 1.2-cm) dog-ear fence panels

23½ x 5½ x ½ in. (59.5 x 14 x 1.2 cm) dog-ear fence for back panel mount

Waterproof glue

1-in. (25-mm) finish nails or galvanized wire nails

10 x 1¼-in. (30-mm) exterior screws (for door and back panel)

1¾-in. (4.5-cm) length of ⁵⁄₁₆-in. (8-mm) round dowel

3 x 2½-in. (60-mm) exterior screws (for mount board)

Painter's putty (optional)

80-grit sandpaper

Light yellow exterior oil-based spray paint

Brown and gray primer oil-based exterior spray paints

Dark brown exterior craft paint

Water-based exterior varnish

Moss and driftwood sticks (optional)

Basic tool kit (see page 132)

finished size

Approx. 16 x 9 x 7½ in. (40.5 x 23 x 19 cm)

Back mount: 23½ in. (59.5 cm)

interior dimensions

Floor area: 6 x 7½ in. (15 x 19 cm)

Cavity depth: 15½ in. 39 cm)

Entrance hole to floor: 13 in. (33 cm)

Entrance hole: 2 in. (5 cm) in diameter

cutting list

Front and back: 16 x 7½ in. (40 x 19 cm)—cut 2

Sides: 14½ x 7½ in. (36 x 19 cm)—cut 2 (one side is reserved for the door)

Roof: 10½ x 7½ in. (26.5 x 19 cm)—cut 2

Floor: 6¼ x 7 in. (16 x 17.7cm)—cut 1

1 Cut the peaks of the front and back panels at a 22.5° angle. Bevel the top edge of the side panels at a 22.5° angle. Cut a 2-in. (5-cm) entrance hole in the front panel, 13½ in. (34 cm) from the bottom and centered on the width. Using a ⁵⁄₁₆-in. (8-mm) bit, drill a drainage hole in the center of the floor panel.

2 Assemble the body of the birdhouse, following steps 2–4 of the Basic Birdhouse on page 9. Drill a hole for the perch and insert a 1¾-in. (4.5-cm) length of round dowel (see step 9 on page 10). Using a ⁵⁄₁₆-in. (8-mm) bit, drill three ventilation holes at an upward angle on the side panel opposite the door.

3 Using 2½-in. (60-mm) exterior screws, attach the birdhouse to the back mount board, positioning it 4½ in. (11.5 cm) from the top. Then, attach the roof, following the instructions for the Simple Roof on page 11.

4 Fill any holes with paintable putty and sand smooth. Place wadded-up paper or tape in the entrance hole to protect the interior.

5 Prime the body of the birdhouse with brown paint and the roof with gray paint. Paint the body of the birdhouse with light yellow paint, then drybrush the roof with dark brown exterior craft paint so that some of the gray shows through, creating a worn effect.

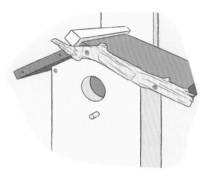

6 If you wish, add driftwood sticks to the front eaves, using small screws to attach them.

7 Dilute 1 part brown exterior craft paint with 3 parts water, then brush it onto the front and sides of the birdhouse, allowing it to trickle down. If you wish, you can use a small piece of rag to drag or dab the paint on. Leave to dry.

8 Varnish the birdhouse (see page 132) and leave to dry. Add a driftwood stick for the door handle and more sticks at the base of the front by drilling through from the inside. Using waterproof glue, attach a little moss to the driftwood sticks.

With its mossy green covering and pieces of driftwood and wood bark, this birdhouse is inspired by Mother Nature. Set it on a patio table or a shelf under a garden porch; alternatively, attach a metal pipe clamp (clip) to the roof as a hanger (see page 138).

moss-covered
birdhouse

materials

One 6 ft x 5½ in. x ½ in. (180 x 14 x 1.2 cm) dog-ear fence panel

Waterproof glue

1-in. (25-mm) finish nails or galvanized wire nails

1¼-in. (30-mm) exterior screws

Paintable wood-filler putty

80-grit sandpaper

Green oil-based exterior spray paint

Self-adhesive moss sheet, available from craft stores

Loose, artificial moss

Driftwood sticks and small wood bark chips

Staples

Basic tool kit (see page 132)

finished size

Approx. 11 x 6⅜ x 5½ in. (28 x 16 x 14 cm)

interior dimensions

Floor area: 4¼ x 5½ in. (11 x 14 cm)

Cavity depth: 9 in. (23 cm)

Entrance hole to floor: 6 in. (15 cm)

Entrance hole: 1½ in. (40 mm) in diameter

cutting list

Front and back: 9¼ x 5½ in. (23.5 x 14 cm)—cut 2

Sides: 6¼ x 5½ in. (16 x 14 cm)—cut 2 (one side is reserved for the door)

Bottom roof: 5 x 5½ in. (13 x 14 cm)—cut 2

Top roof: 5¾ x 5½ in. (14.5 x 14 cm)—cut 2

Floor: 4¼ x 5½ in. (11 x 14 cm)—cut 1

1 Referring to the Basic Birdhouse on page 8, cut and shape the birdhouse pieces from dog-ear fence board. Cut a 1½-in. (40-mm) entrance hole, 6½ in. (16.5 cm) from the bottom of the front panel and centered on the width.

2 Assemble the birdhouse, following steps 2–8 of the Basic Birdhouse on pages 9–10. Prepare the birdhouse for painting (see step 10 on page 10), then paint green and leave to dry. Lightly sand.

3 Cut the self-adhesive moss sheet to size, peel off the backing, and apply to the birdhouse one panel at a time, making sure you don't cover the sides of the door. Use a utility knife to cut a slit in the moss over the front entrance hole, then push the moss through to the inside with your fingers. Glue loose moss into any gaps, then staple the moss around the edges of the birdhouse to fix it securely.

4 Pre-drill holes in driftwood sticks, then screw the sticks onto the roof and box. Remember to attach a piece of driftwood for the door knob. Apply a generous amount of glue to the roof and cover with loose moss and small pieces of bark, pressing the moss down firmly to ensure that it sticks.

House Sparrow

Simple birdhouses joined together make a classic condo for birds to enjoy. I chose three different shades of enticing blue for my condo, but you could make each birdhouse a completely different color if you prefer. I used pieces of driftwood as embellishments, as I love using "found" objects as decoration and I think they give the birdhouses a lovely rustic feel—but the type and amount of decoration you add is entirely up to you.

birdhouse trio

materials

One 6 ft x 7½ in. x ½ in. (180 x 19 x 1.2 cm) dog-ear fence panel

Two 6 ft x 5½ in. x ½ in. (180 x 14 x 1.2 cm) dog-ear fence panels

Waterproof glue

1-in. (25-mm) finish nails or galvanized wire nails

10 x 1¼-in. (30-mm) exterior screws

Three 1¾-in. (4.5-cm) lengths of ⁵⁄₁₆-in. (8-mm) round dowel for perches

Driftwood sticks

Paintable wood-filler putty

80-grit sandpaper

Oil-based exterior spray paints in three shades of blue (or your chosen color)

Dark brown and dark green exterior craft paints

Water-based exterior varnish

Basic tool kit (see page 132)

finished size

Approx. 8½ x 19½ x 5½ in. (21.5 x 49.5 x 14 cm)

interior dimensions

Floor area: 4¼ x 5½ in. (10.75 x 14 cm)

Cavity depth: 8 in. (20 cm)

Entrance hole to floor: 6 in. (15 cm)

Entrance hole: 1½ in. (4 cm) in diameter

cutting list

Front panel (door): 8 x 5½ in. (20 x 14 cm)—cut 1 for each box

Back panel: 8½ x 5½ in. (21.5 x 14 cm)—cut 1 for each box

Side panels: 8¾ x 5½ in. (22.3 x 14 cm)—cut 2 for each box

Floor: 4¼ x 5½ in. (11 x 14 cm)—cut 1 for each box

Side roof panels: 6½ x 7½ in. (16.5 x 19 cm)—cut 2

Center roof panel: 9 x 7½ in. (23 x 19 cm)—cut 1

1 Referring to the Basic Birdhouse on page 8, cut the birdhouse pieces from dog-ear fence board. Cut the top edges of the side panels at a 15° angle. Bevel the top edges of the front and back panels at 15°. Cut a 1½-in. (4-cm) entrance hole, 1½ in. (4 cm) from the top of each front panel and centered on the width.

2 Following steps 2–4 of the Basic Birdhouse on page 9, assemble the bodies of the three birdhouses; the tallest side of the side panels should align with the back panel, while the front panel – the door – will overhang at the base by 1 in. (2.5 cm). On each front panel, drill a hole 1 in. (2.5 cm) below the entrance hole and insert a length of round dowel for the perch (see step 9 on page 10). Remove the front panels (the doors) of all three boxes, as this makes it easier to join them together.

3 On the box that will go in the middle of the condo, using a speed square, draw a straight line vertically down the center of each side. Now measure 3½ in. (9 cm) up the center line from the base and draw a line from here to the front edge. The other two boxes will attach at these points. Using a ⅛-in. (3-mm) bit, drill two pilot holes (see page 136) through the side panels of the outer and center boxes from the inside and insert 1¼-in. (30-mm) screws.

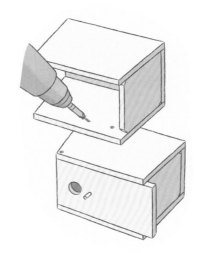

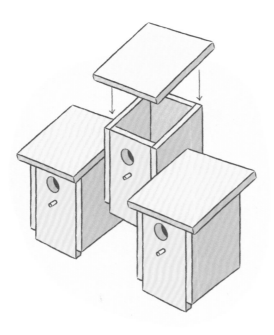

4 Glue and nail the roofs of the two outer boxes in place, flush with the sides of the center box and overhanging on the other three sides. Glue and nail the center roof panel to the middle box, overhanging by the same amount on all four sides. Re-attach the three door panels.

5 Prepare the birdhouse for painting (see step 10 on page 10). Paint the body of each birdhouse in a different shade of blue (or color of your choice). Paint the roofs and their edges dark brown.

6 While the brown paint is still wet, brush streaks of dark green across from back to front to create the impression of moss growing on the roof. Wipe off any excess paint if necessary, taking care to wipe in the same direction as your brushstrokes. Leave to dry, then varnish the exterior of the birdhouses (see page 132).

7 Lay the assembled birdhouse on your work surface with the front facing up. Place driftwood sticks on top to check the position, making sure that the doors will open once they are attached. Remove the doors one at a time. Drill pilot holes (see page 136) from the back, then screw the driftwood pieces in place. Attach sticks to the top of the middle birdhouse roof in the same way, then replace the doors.

8 Place the birdhouse on a patio or sturdy, level wall. Alternatively, you could mount it on a post (see page 137). Mounting birdhouses on galvanized steel poles is the best way to keep predators from climbing up in search of young nestlings or fledglings. You can find the poles and everything you need to attach the birdhouse to them in the fencing and electrical departments of your local home-improvement store.

chapter 2

modern birdhouses

While some people like their birdhouses to have a rustic look, there's
always room for those who like straight lines, bold colors, and
unusual shapes. Here you'll find stylish and fun ideas, from
a colorful two-storey condo and a "townhouse" decorated with
miniature tiles, to an industrial-style birdhouse with simple
lines and eclectic embellishments.

Accented with a blue hummingbird pendant, this beautifully ornate birdhouse is decorated with glass tiles and a metal roof and would suit a beach or waterfront home perfectly. It is easily attached to a tree, a fence, or the side of a wooden house by means of a back mount panel.

mosaic tiled birdhouse
with pendant

Dark-Eyed Junco

materials

One 6 ft x 5½ in. 2½ in. (180 x 14 x 1.2 cm) dog-ear fence board

One 6 ft x 4 in. x 1 in. (180 x 10 x 2.5 cm) piece of lumber (timber)

Waterproof glue

1-in. (25-mm) finish nails or galvanized wire nails

12 x ¾-in. (20-mm) wood screws

80-grit sandpaper

White oil-based primer paint

Light blue oil-based exterior spray paint

Light blue exterior craft paint

Two 12 x 12-in. (30 x 30-cm) sheets of small mosaic (meshed) glass tiles

Waterproof silicone glue

Gray grout

6 x 1¼-in. (30-mm) exterior screws

2 x 2-in. (50-mm) exterior screws for mount panel

12 x 8 in. (20 x 20 cm) steel roof flashing (from home improvement store)

1¾-in. (4.5-cm) length of round dowel, ¼ in. (6 mm) in diameter, for perch

Dark blue glass knob, 1½ in. (4 cm) in diameter

Hummingbird pendant, approx. 2½ x 1¾ in. (6 x 4.5 cm)

2 in. (5 cm) heavy wire

Basic tool kit (see page 132)

finished size

Approx. 16 x 8 x 9 in. (40 x 20 x 23 cm)

interior dimensions

Floor area: 4¼ x 5½ in. (10.75 x 14 cm)

Cavity depth: 10 in. (25 cm)

Entrance hole to floor: 8 in. (20 cm)

Entrance hole: 1½ in. (40 mm) in diameter

cutting list

Front and back: 12 x 5½ in. (30 x 14 cm)—cut 2

Sides: 9¼ x 5½ in. (23.5 x 14 cm)—cut 2 (one side is reserved for the door)

Floor: 4¼ x 5½ in. (10.75 x 14 cm)—cut 1

Roof: 8 x 5½ in. (20 x 14 cm)—cut 2

1 Referring to the Basic Birdhouse on page 8, cut the birdhouse pieces from dog-ear fence board and shape them. Cut the peaks of the front and back panels at a 45° angle. Bevel the top edges of the side panels at a 45° angle. Do not bevel the roof panels. Cut ¼ in. (6 mm) diagonally off each corner of the floor panel. Cut a 1½-in. (40-mm) entrance hole in the front panel, 8½ in. (21.5 cm) from the bottom and centered on the width.

2 Assemble the body of the birdhouse, following steps 2–4 of the Basic Birdhouse on page 9. Glue and nail the two roof panels together, then glue and nail the roof to the birdhouse, flush with the back edge. The roof will overhang at the front to protect the entrance hole from rain.

3 Prepare the birdhouse for painting (see step 10 on page 10), then paint with white oil-based primer.

4 From lumber (timber), cut one back mount panel measuring 16 in. x 4 in. (40 x 10 cm). Cut off each end at a 45° angle, 1¼ in. (3 cm) from the edge, to make a dog-ear shape. Using a ⅛-in. (3-mm) bit, drill pilot holes 1 in. (2.5 cm) in from each side and ¾ in. (2 cm) down from the top. Drill in 2-in. (50-mm) exterior screws to attach the mount panel to a post or tree when the birdhouse is complete.

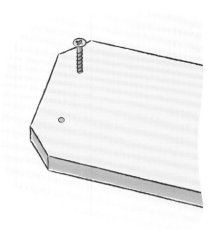

5 Paint the front and back of the mount panel with light blue oil-based exterior spray paint. Using a ⅛-in. (3-mm) bit, drill four pilot holes in the mount panel (see page 136), then drill in 1¼-in. (30-mm) screws to attach the back mount panel to the center of the back of the birdhouse.

6 Dry fit a sheet of mosaic (meshed) tile over the front, then cut to size with a utility knife by cutting through the mesh on the back of the tiles. Remove any tiles that hit the underside of the roof and save all the cut-off pieces for use later. Cut out a square of tiles around the entrance hole, and remove any tiles that cover up the screws attaching the door to the front panel.

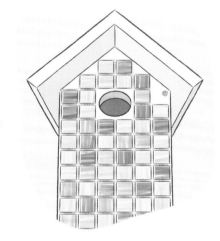

7 Using a pencil, draw around the outline of the tile sheet on the birdhouse. Lift off the tiles. Apply waterproof silicone glue inside your pencil marks and put the tile sheet in place. Fill in any gaps using the tile off-cuts from step 6. The silicone will bond quickly, but you will still have time to move the tiles and off-cuts around to get them to fit.

8 Repeat on the sides of the birdhouse, making sure that the door will still open and close properly when the tiles are in position. Remove tiles from where the door knob will go. Drill a 3/16-in. (5-mm) hole and attach the door knob. Fill in any gaps using off-cuts from step 6.

9 Apply tiles to the front roof fascia; don't worry if you have space at the end, as you will fill it with grout later.

10 Put on gloves to protect your hands. Find the center of the steel flashing, place it on the edge of a table and press. Place the crease on the center of the roof and press it down flush with the roof panels.

11 Using a ⅟₁₆-in. (1.5-mm) bit, drill tiny indentations in the flashing along the lower edge of the roof, ¼ in. (6 mm) up from the edge and 4 in. (10 cm) apart. Change to a ⅛-in. (3-mm) bit and drill in ¾-in. (20-mm) wood screws to attach the flashing to the roof. Repeat along the ridge of the roof, spacing the screws 1¼ in. (3 cm) from the ridge, then repeat on the other side of the roof. Using flat-nose pliers, crimp the ridge of the roof, so that the flashing sits tight against the roof panels.

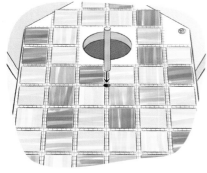

12 Using a ¼-in. (6-mm) bit, drill a hole in between two tiles about 1 in. (2.5 cm) below the entrance hole. Tap in a 1¾-in. (4.5-cm) length of round dowel for the perch.

13 Using a metal or rubber spatula, apply pre-mixed grout over the tiles, pressing it into each gap and around the entrance hole. Repeat on the sides and roof fascia, making sure you keep the door edges and opening free of grout. Leave for a few minutes (follow the instructions on the tub), then wipe with a damp sponge to smooth out the grout. Once the grout has dried firmly (about 15 minutes—but check the manufacturer's instructions), wipe off any film that has formed on the surface with a damp sponge.

14 Decide where you want the hummingbird pendant to go and drill a ⅛-in. (3-mm) hole between two tiles at this point. Thread a length of wire through the loop on the back of the pendant and twist the ends together. Using a toothpick, apply a tiny dab of silicone glue to the inside of the hole, then press the wires onto the glue to secure, making sure they do not stick through to the inside of the birdhouse.

15 Paint the base of the birdhouse in light blue exterior craft paint, to match the back mount panel. Apply the same color in any other places where the primer shows through. You do not need to varnish this birdhouse, as the grout will have waterproof sealant in it.

Look around the house to find objects that will work outside in harsh weather. In this utilitarian-looking "outhouse," the combination of gray primer and a dragged ivory topcoat creates a metallic effect, while the decorative screws and spring-like twists of wire enhance the industrial feel.

outhouse birdhouse

materials

One 6 ft x 5½ in. x ½ in. (180 x 14 x 1.2 cm) dog-ear fence panel

One 6 ft x 7½ in. x ½ in. (180 x 19 x 1.2 cm) dog-ear fence panel for roof

Waterproof glue

1-in. (25-mm) finish nails or galvanized wire nails

2 x 2-in. (50-mm) exterior screws

6 x 1¼-in. (30-mm) exterior screws

One 1¾-in. (4.5-cm) and two 1-in. (2.5-cm) lengths of ⁵⁄₁₆-in. (8-mm) round dowel for perches

Paintable wood-filler putty

80-grit sandpaper

Gray oil-based exterior primer spray paint

Ivory oil-based exterior spray paint

Brown and dark green exterior craft paint

1-in. (2.5-cm) ball drawer knob

Black washer, metal screw bolts, and heavy wire for embellishments

One 19 x 3 x 1 in. (48 x 7.5 x 2.5 cm) piece of lumber (timber) for back mount panel

Water-based exterior varnish

Basic tool kit (see page 132)

finished size

Approx. 15 x 5½ x 7 in. (38 x 14 x 18 cm)

Back mount panel: 19 in. (48 cm)

interior dimensions

Floor area: 4¼ x 5½ in. (11 x 14 cm)

Cavity depth: 11 in. (28 cm)

Entrance hole to floor: 9½ in. (24 cm)

Entrance hole: 1¼ in. (32 mm) diameter

cutting list

Front and back: 14½ x 5½ in. (36.5 x 14 cm)—cut 2

Side panel 1: 8¾ x 5½ in. (24 x 14 cm)—cut 1 (this will be the door)

Side panel 2: 14 x 5½ in. (35.5 x 14 cm)—cut 1

Roof: 12 x 5½ in. (30 x 14 cm)—cut 1

Floor: 4¼ x 5½ in. (11 x 14 cm)—cut 1

Back mount panel: 19 x 3 in. (48 x 7.5 cm)—cut 1 from lumber (timber)

1 Referring to the Basic Birdhouse on pages 8–10, cut the birdhouse pieces from dog-ear fence board. Draw a pencil line at a 45° angle from the top right of the front and back panels to the left–hand side and miter cut, so that the left-hand side is 9 in. (23 cm) tall. Bevel the top edges of each side panel at 45°.

2 Assemble the body of the birdhouse, following steps 2–4 of the Basic Birdhouse on page 9.

3 Bevel one short end of the roof panel at a 45° angle. At the other end of the roof panel, make a pencil mark on the left-hand side, 3 in. (7.5 cm) down from the top edge. Draw a line from this point to the top edge at a 45° angle, then cut along the line.

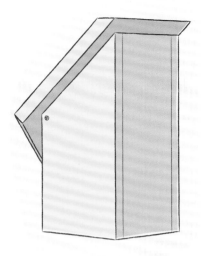

4 With the beveled edge at the top, facing up, glue and nail the roof panel in place, flush with the back panel and overlapping the tall side panel by 1 in. (2.5 cm). The panel will overhang by 3 in. (7.5 cm) at the lower side and ½ in. (1 cm) at the front.

5 In the front panel, cut a 1¼-in. (32-mm) entrance hole about 1 in. (2.5 cm) from the side and 1½ in. (4 cm) below the roof. Using a ⁵⁄₁₆-in. (8-mm) bit, drill three holes for dowel perches below the entrance hole. Gently tap in the perches (see step 9 on page 10), inserting the longest perch in the right-hand hole. ⁵⁄₁₆-in. (8-mm)

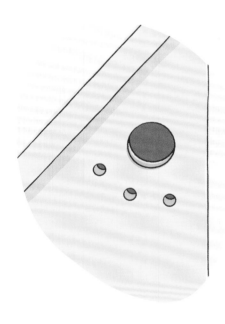

6 Using a ⁵⁄₁₆-in. (8-mm) bit, drill ventilation holes at the back of the birdhouse, 1½ in. (4 cm) under the eaves, slanting them slightly upward to prevent water from seeping in.

7 Cut one short end of the mount panel at a 45° angle. Drill holes for 2-in. (50-mm) screws at the top. Attach the mount panel to the center of the back panel of the birdhouse, aligning the straight end with the bottom of the birdhouse.

8 Cut a 2¼ x 5½-in. (5.7 x 14-cm) piece of scrap fence panel for a fake "door." Glue and nail it to the front of the birdhouse.

9 Drill a hole through from the back of the door for the door knob, then attach the door knob with a 1¼-in. (30-mm) screw.

10 Prime the birdhouse with gray paint and leave to dry. Apply ivory paint to the front panel. While it is still wet, drag a spatula down the panel from top to bottom to create textured marks like wood grain. Repeat on the side panels, allowing each side to dry before you paint the next one.

11 Dilute one part dark brown craft paint to three parts water, and brush onto the roof and edges. While the brown paint is still slightly wet, mix one part green craft paint to three parts water, put in a small plastic bottle, and lightly trickle over the roof to create a weathered, mossy effect, dabbing off excess paint with a rag, if necessary. Repeat this process on the door knob and front "door" panel. Paint the dowel perches in watered-down brown craft paint. Leave to dry.

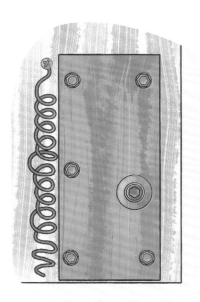

12 Embellish the front "door" with a metal washer for the door knob, colored screw bolts, and twists of wire.

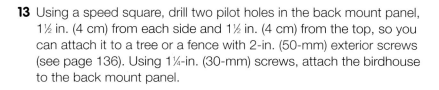

Marsh Tit

13 Using a speed square, drill two pilot holes in the back mount panel, 1½ in. (4 cm) from each side and 1½ in. (4 cm) from the top, so you can attach it to a tree or a fence with 2-in. (50-mm) exterior screws (see page 136). Using 1¼-in. (30-mm) screws, attach the birdhouse to the back mount panel.

14 Varnish the exterior of the birdhouse and the back mount panel (see page 132).

Reminiscent of a loft apartment in the Hollywood Hills, this birdhouse is painted bright red, with glass circles serving as "windows." Birds will be flocking to live here! The side hut lifts up to reveal the clean-out door.

designer birdhouse

materials

Two 6 ft x 5½ in. x ½ in. (180 x 14 x 1.2 cm) dog-ear fence panels

Waterproof glue

1-in. (25-mm) finish nails or galvanized wire nails

4 x 2½-in. (60-mm) exterior screws (for mounting bracket)

5 x 1¼-in. (30-mm) exterior screws

Two 1-in. (2.5-cm) and one 1¾-in. (4.5-cm) lengths of ⁵⁄₁₆-in. (8-mm) round dowel for perches

Paintable wood-filler putty

80-grit sandpaper

Exterior craft paint in dark brown and three shades of green

Red oil-based exterior spray paint

5 flat-backed, circular glass beads, 1 in. (2.5 cm) in diameter

Green craft wire

Water-based exterior varnish

Basic tool kit (see page 132)

finished size

Approx. 19 x 12 x 8½ in. (48 x 30 x 21.5 cm)

interior dimensions

Floor area: 4¼ x 5½ in. (10.5 x 14 cm)

Cavity depth: 10 in. (25 cm)

Entrance hole to floor: 8 in. (20 cm)

Entrance hole: 1½ in. (40 mm) in diameter

cutting list

MAIN BIRDHOUSE

Front and back: 12¼ x 5½ in. (30 x 14 cm)—cut 2 front panels and 1 back panel

Side panel 1: 8½ x 5½ in. (21.5 x 14 cm)—cut 1

Side panel 2: 10¾ x 5½ in. (27.25 x 14 cm)—cut 1 (this will be the door)

Bottom roof panel 1: 6 x 5½ in. (15 x 14 cm)—cut 1

Bottom roof panel 2: 3¾ x 5½ in. (9.5 x 14 cm)—cut 1

Top roof panel 1: 6¼ x 5½ in. (15.5 x 14 cm)—cut 1

Top roof panel 2: 3¾ x 5½ in. (9.5 x 14 cm)—cut 1

Floor: 4¼ x 5½ in. (11 x 14 cm)—cut 1

SIDE HUT

Roof panel: 7½ in. x 5½ in. (19 x 14 cm)—cut 1 from the dog-ear end of the fence panel

Floor: 2½ in. (6 cm) square

Side panel: 4 x 5½ in. (10 x 14 cm)

FRONT FAÇADE

Front façade panel: 12¼ x 5½ in. (30 x 14 cm)—cut 1

Left roof trim: 2 x 1½ in, (5 x 4 cm)—cut 1

Right roof trim: 5½ x 1½ in. (14 x 4 cm)—cut 1

---

1 Referring to the Basic Birdhouse on page 8, cut the main birdhouse pieces from dog-ear fence board. Mark a point on the top edge of the front and back panels, 2 in. (5 cm) from the left-hand side. Cut from this point to the side edges at a 45° angle to create the asymmetrically shaped roof. Cut a 1½-in. (40-mm) hole in one front panel, 8½ in. (21.5 cm) from the base and ¾ in. (2 cm) from the side. (The second front panel will be used later for the lower front façade; see step 6.)

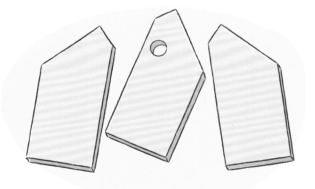

2 Cut and shape the side, roof, and floor pieces of the main birdhouse, following the instructions for the Basic Birdhouse on page 8.

3 Assemble the main birdhouse, following steps 1–9 of the Basic Birdhouse on pages 9–10. (Remember to turn the back panel over, so that the asymmetrical roof aligns with the roof of the front.) Using a ⁵⁄₁₆-in. (8-mm) bit, drill a hole in the front panel hole for the dowel perch, centering it 1 in. (2.5 cm) below the entrance hole, and insert the perch (see step 9 on page 10).

4 Remove the door to make the side hut. Bevel the side-hut roof panel at 45° on the end opposite the dog ear. Bevel one end of the hut side panel at 45°. Glue and nail the side-hut roof panel to the door of the main birdhouse, 3 in. (7.5 cm) from the top edge. Glue and nail the hut side panel to the roof panel of the side hut, then glue and nail the floor panel between the side panel and the main birdhouse door.

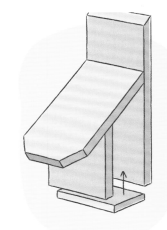

5 Place the open side of the side hut on a piece of paper and draw around the inside to make a template. Using the template, cut one front and one back panel to this size. In the front panel, cut a 1-in. (2.5-cm) hole, 3 in. (7.5 cm) from the base and 1½ in. (4 cm) from the left-hand edge. Drill a hole for the perch 1 in. (2.5 cm) below the hole then insert the perch. Glue and nail them to the open sides of the side hut. Re-attach the main birdhouse door panel to the main birdhouse.

6 Cut and shape the lower front façade in the same way as the front panel of the main birdhouse, then cut a 1-in. (2.5-cm hole) 8½ in. (21.5 cm) from the bottom and ¾ in. (2 cm) from the left-hand side. Drill a hole for the perch 1 in. (2.5 cm) below and slightly to the right of the hole, then insert the perch. Glue and nail the roof trim panels to the front façade, flush with the back edge.

7 Using a ⅛-in. (3-mm) bit, drill three pilot holes 2 in. (5 cm) apart just below the roof trim of the front façade, then attach the façade to the front of the main birdhouse, using 1¼-in. (30-mm) screws; the façade should extend 6 in. (15 cm) below the main birdhouse.

8 Using a speed square, mark four spots on the lower front façade 2 and 4 in. (5 and 10 cm) from the bottom and 2 in. (5 cm) in from each side.

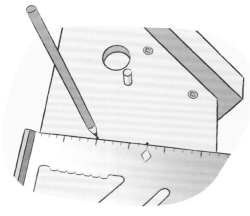

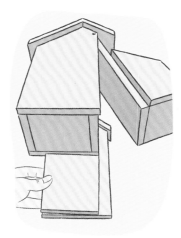

9 Cut a 4 x 5-in. (10 x 12.5-cm) piece of fence panel. Glue and nail it to the back of the façade, butting up against the floor of the main birdhouse; this is to make the façade stronger, so that you can attach it to the mount post. Using a ⅛-in. (3-mm) bit, drill pilot holes at the four points you marked in the previous step and countersink 2½-in. (60-mm) screws using a ¾-in. (20-mm) bit (see page 135).

10 Mask off the entrance hole, then paint the entire birdhouse red. Leave to dry. Next, mask off the sides, then paint the roof green. Load your brush with two shades of green exterior craft paint, then dab it onto the roof panels, dipping the brush into a third shade of green from time to time to enhance the texture and weathered look. Leave to dry. Using a rag, dab on brown exterior craft paint in places to get a mottled effect.

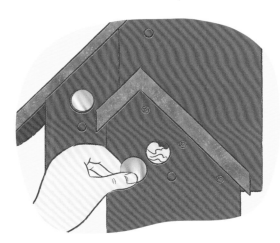

11 Apply clear silicone adhesive to the 1-in. (2.5-cm) holes in the front façade and the front of the side hut and press a circular glass bead into each one.

12 Cut an 8-in. (20-cm) length of green craft wire. Thread it through one of the remaining glass beads, then bring the wire around the back of the bead and twist both ends together two or three times above the bead. Curl the remaining wire around a pencil, leaving 2 in. (5 cm) uncurled. Using a ⁷⁄₃₂-in. (5-mm) bit, drill holes about 2 in. (5 cm) apart in the eaves of the main birdhouse. Push the wires through from under the eaves, then twist the straight ends with pliers to stop them from falling out of the holes.

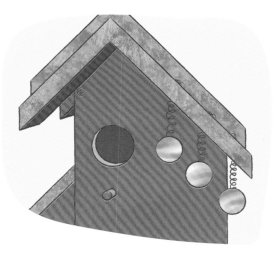

13 Varnish the exterior of the birdhouse (see page 132). Mount the birdhouse on a 4 x 4-in. (10 x 10-cm) post (see page 137).

With its sleek lines and metal embellishments, this birdhouse has a clean, modern, industrial look. The metal embellishments can be found in the building section of your local home improvement store; you can paint the metal roof with oil-based exterior paint if you wish, or leave it unpainted, as I did.

industrial **birdhouse**

materials

One 6 ft x 5½ in. x ½ in. (180 x 14 x 1.2 cm) dog-ear fence board

Waterproof glue

1-in. (25-mm) finish nails or galvanized wire nails

28 x ¾-in. (20-mm) wood screws

2 x 1¼-in. (30-mm) exterior screws

1¾-in. (4.5-cm) length of ⁵⁄₁₆-in. (8-mm) round dowel for perch

80-grit sandpaper

Dark blue oil-based exterior spray paint

8 x 12-in. (20 x 30-cm) steel roof flashing (found in roofing section)

Key ring

Swivel pail paint hook

Two-hole steel D-ring hanger for door pull

Metal L-brackets, lengths of chain, two-hole connector and other embellishments of your choice

Water-based exterior varnish

Basic tool kit (see page 132)

finished size

Approx. 10 x 5½ x 5¼ in. (25 x 14 x 13.5 cm)

interior dimensions

Floor area: 4 x 4 in. (10 x 10 cm)

Cavity depth: 9 in. (23 cm)

Entrance hole to floor: 5 in. (12.5 cm)

Entrance hole: 1⅛ in. (28 mm) in diameter

cutting list

Front and back: 12 x 5½ in. (30 x 14 cm)—cut 2

Side 1: 6¾ x 4 in. (17.2 x 10 cm) —cut 1 for door

Side 2: 8½ x 4 in. (21.5 x 14 cm)—cut 1

Floor: 4 x 5 in. (10 x 10 cm)

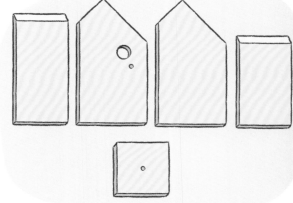

1 Referring to the Basic Birdhouse on page 8, cut the birdhouse pieces from dog-ear fence board. Cut across the top of the front and back panels at 45°, then make a 45° cut 2½ in. (6 cm) long on the opposite side. Bevel one short end of each side panel at 45°. Drill a ⁵⁄₁₆-in. (8-mm) hole in the center of the floor panel for drainage. Cut a 1⅛-in. (28-mm) entrance hole, 5½ in. (14 cm) from the bottom of the front panel and 1¼ in. (3.2 cm) from the side. Cut a ⁵⁄₁₆-in. (8-mm) hole in the front panel for the perch 1 in. (2.5 cm) down from the entrance hole and 1 in. (2.5 cm) from the side.

2 Assemble the body of the birdhouse, following steps 2–4 of the Basic Birdhouse on page 8. Prepare the birdhouse for painting (see step 10 on page 10), then spray with bright blue exterior spray paint.

3 Put on gloves to protect your hands. Remove the sharp edges from the metal flashing by curling the corners inward with a pair of needle-nose pliers. Bend the flashing in half over the roof ridge. Mark where each screw needs to go with a black marker pen. Using a ⅛-in. (3-mm) bit, drill pilot holes through the metal 1 in. (2.5-cm) down from the top ridge on each side; add a second row if you feel it is necessary. Screw in ¾-in. (20-mm) wood screws. Using flat-nose pliers, crimp the ridge of the roof, so that the flashing sits tight against the roof panels.

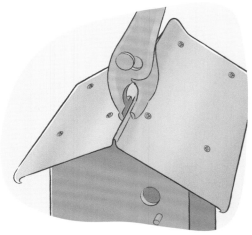

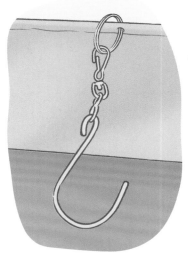

4 Using a ⅛-in. (3-mm) bit, drill holes on each side of the roof ridge and insert a metal keyring. Attach a swivel-pail paint hook (available in the paint department of your local home improvement store), ready to hang.

5 Using a 1/16-in. (1.5-mm) bit, drill pilot holes in the door and attach a two-hole steel D-ring hanger for the door pull, using ¾-in. (20-mm) wood screws.

6 Using 1/16-in. (1.5-mm) bit, drill pilot holes in the side and door panels and attach your chosen metal embellishments with ¾-in. (20-mm) wood screws. I used L-brackets and a small two-hole connector, and a length of chain, which I attached by partially unscrewing one screw in each bracket, clamping the end of the chain underneath, and tightening the screws again.

7 Varnish the wooden parts of the birdhouse (see page 132).

This unique birdhouse will accommodate birds that nest in open wall boxes. The sides are left open enough for easy exit and nest removal once the youngsters have fledged. Birds that use these nests commonly weave their nesting baskets in a hanging flower pot, open rocks, or sparse bush. It's great for birds that find a nesting spot under a porch pillar.

birdhouse
bungalow

materials

One 6 ft x 5½ in. x ½ in. (180 x 14 x 1.2 cm) dog-ear fence board

Waterproof glue

1-in. (25-mm) finish nails or galvanized wire nails

4 x 1¼-in. (30-mm) exterior screws

2 x 2-in. (50-mm) exterior screws

Two 1-in. (2.5-cm) and one 1¾-in. (4.5-cm) lengths dowel, ⁵⁄₁₆ in. (8 mm) in diameter, for perches

Paintable wood-filler putty

80-grit sandpaper

Bright yellow and red oil-based exterior spray paints

Red and green exterior craft paint

4 packs of shims

⅝-in. (6-mm) wire brads

Small stick, approx. 3 in. (7.5 cm) long

Moss

Water-based exterior varnish

Basic tool kit (see page 132)

finished size

Approx. 7¼ x 7½ x 9 in. (18.5 x 19 x 23 cm)

Back mount panel: 14 in. (35.5 cm)

interior dimensions

Floor area: 5¼ x 5½ in. (13.5 x 14 cm)

Cavity depth: 8½ in. (21.5 cm)

Entrance hole to floor: 6 in. (15 cm)

Entrance hole: 1½ in. (40 mm) in diameter

cutting list

Front and back: 9 x 5½ in. (23 x 14 cm) —cut 2

Sides: 6½ x 5½ in. (16.5 x 14 cm)—cut 2

Roof: 8 x 5½ in. (20 x 14 cm)—cut 2

Floor: 5¼ x 5½ in. (13.5 x 14 cm)—cut 1

Back mount panel: 14 in. (35.5 cm)— cut 1 from the dog-ear end of the fence panel

1 Referring to the Basic Birdhouse on page 8, cut the birdhouse pieces from dog-ear fence board. Cut the peaks of the front and back panels at a 15° angle. Cut a 1½-in. (40-mm) entrance hole, 1½ in. (4 cm) from the top of the front panel and centered on the width.

2 Glue and nail the side panels to the outside edges of the front and back panels, aligning them at the base. Glue and nail the floor panel in place.

3 Glue and nail the roof panels onto the front and back panels, flush with the back panel and overhanging the front by 1½ in. (4 cm), leaving a V-shaped gap in the center. Drill three holes for the dowel perches where shown, using a ⁵⁄₁₆-in. (8-mm) drill bit. Insert the perches into the holes, hammering the 1¾-in. (4.5-cm) length into the hole below the entrance hole and the 1-in. (2.5-cm) lengths into the other holes.

4 Prepare the birdhouse for painting (see step 10, page 10), then paint the birdhouse bright yellow.

5 Using a speed square, mark and pre-drill screw two holes in the back mount panel, 1½ in. (4 cm) from each side and 1½ in. (4 cm) from the top, so you can attach it to a tree or fence with 2-in. (50-mm) exterior screws. Paint the back mount panel bright yellow.

6 Using 1¼-in. (30-mm) screws, attach the birdhouse to the back mount panel.

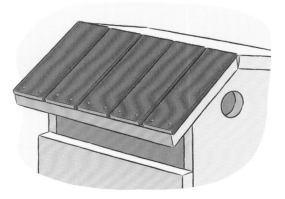

7 Paint the shims red on both sides and leave to dry. Cut the first row of shims to fit across each side of the roof, from eave to ridge. Using a ¹⁄₁₆-in. (1.5-mm) pin bit, pre-drill holes at the top and bottom or each shim and gently hammer in wire brad nails. Apply two more rows on shims in the same way, cutting each one about 1½ in. (4 cm) shorter than the previous one and aligning one end with the ridge of the roof.

8 Paint the dowel perches with green exterior craft paint and leave to dry.

9 Add shims to the front and sides, staggering the lengths as shown. Touch up the raw cut edges of the shims with red exterior craft paint.

10 Drill a pilot hole through a small stick. Using a 1-in. finish nail, attach the stick to the roof, above the entrance hole. Glue a little moss behind the stick and to the roof ridge.

11 Plug the entrance hole with wadded-up paper or tape, then varnish the exterior of the birdhouse (see page 132).

With its yellow squares on a dark purple base, this birdhouse has a definite retro feel! Using a checkerboard stencil is a fun and easy way to dress up any project.

checkerboard
birdhouse

materials

One 6 ft x 5½ in. x ½ in. (180 x 14 x 1.2 cm) dog-ear fence panel

One 6 ft x 7½ in. x ½ in. (180 x 19 x 1.2 cm) dog-ear fence panel

Waterproof glue

1-in. (25-mm) finish nails or galvanized wire nails

1¾-in. (4.5-cm) length of ⁵⁄₁₆-in. (8-mm) round dowel for perch

4 x ¾-in. (20-mm) machine screws

6 x 1¼-in. (30-mm) exterior screws

2 x 2½-in. (60-mm) exterior screws

Paintable wood-filler putty

80-grit sandpaper

Stencil with checkerboard design

Masking tape

Dark purple oil-based exterior spray paint

Yellow exterior craft paint

Water-based exterior varnish

Basic tool kit (see page 132)

Finished size

Approx. 6½ x 6¼ x 7½ in. (16.5 x 16 x 19 cm)

Interior dimensions

Floor area: 4¼ x 5½ in. (11 x 14 cm)

Cavity depth: 8 in. (20 cm)

Entrance hole to floor: 6 in. (15 cm)

Entrance hole: 1½ in. (40 mm) in diameter

cutting list

Back panel: 12 x 5½ in. (30 x 14 cm)— cut 1

Front panel: 9 x 5½ in. (23 x 14 cm)— cut 1

Side panels: 11 x 5½ in. (29 x 14 cm)— cut 2

Floor: 4¼ x 5½ in. (11 x 14 cm)

Platform roof: 9 x 7½ in. (23 x 19 cm)— cut 1

Back plate: 11 x 7½ in. (28 x 19 cm)— cut 1

1 Referring to the Basic Birdhouse on page 8, cut the birdhouse pieces from dog-ear fence board. Bevel the top edges of the front and back panels at 22.5°. Cut the top edges of the side panels at a 22.5° angle. Cut a 1½-in. (40-mm) entrance hole, 6 in. (15 cm) from the bottom of the front panel and centered on the width. Drill a hole and insert a length of round dowel for the perch 1 in. (2.5 cm) below the entrance hole (see step 9 on page 10).

2 Assemble the body of the birdhouse, following steps 2–4 of the Basic Birdhouse on page 9 as a guide, but note that the front panel is the door on this birdhouse. Glue and nail the roof panel in place, overhanging the back panel by ½ in. (1 cm).

3 Glue and screw in the back plate, with the top edge flush with the back panel and the sides overhanging by 1 in. (2.5 cm), for extra strength. Remove the door. Using a ⅛-in. (3-mm) bit, drill pilot holes (see page 136) through the back panel and back plate for mounting. Drill in 2½-in. (60-mm) screws. Replace the door.

4 Using a ⁵⁄₁₆-in. (8-mm) bit, drill ventilation holes in the side panels just under the eaves, sloping upward to prevent rain from getting in.

5 Prepare the birdhouse for painting (see step 10 on page 10). Paint the whole birdhouse dark purple, then leave to dry. Tape a checkerboard stencil to the front of the birdhouse. Using a stiff-bristled brush or a stencil brush, dry brush yellow exterior craft paint through the stencil to create the pattern. Repeat on the side and front edges of the roof.

Here's a birdhouse that will accommodate two families of wrens or any of the small cavity-nesting birds that will nest in manmade houses. This stylish home would work well in a beach setting. The back mount panel can be omitted if you prefer.

two-storey birdhouse condo

materials

Two 6 ft x 5½ in. x ½ in. (180 x 14 x 1.2 cm) dog-ear fence boards

Waterproof glue

1-in. (25-mm) finish nails or galvanized wire nails

7 x 1¼-in. (30-mm) exterior screws

Two 1¾-in. (4.5-cm) and four 1-in. (2.5-cm) lengths of ⁵⁄₁₆-in. (8-mm) round dowel for perches

Paintable wood-filler putty

80-grit sandpaper

Painter's tape

Brown wood primer paint

Navy blue, ivory, and hammered copper oil-based exterior spray paints

Antique gold metallic, hunter green, and bright yellow exterior craft paints

One 29½ x 3½ x 1-in. (75 x 9 x 2.5-cm) piece of lumber (timber) for back mount panel

2 x 2-in. (50-mm) exterior screws

Basic tool kit (see page 132)

finished size

Approx. 24 x 9 x 5½ in. (61 x 23 x 14 cm)

interior dimensions

Floor area: 4¼ x 5½ in. (11 x 14 cm) each storey

Cavity depth: 10 in./25 cm (top storey); 9 in./23 cm (bottom storey)

Entrance hole to floor: 9 in. (20 cm) each storey

Entrance hole: 1¼ in. (32 mm) in diameter each storey

cutting list

Front and back: 22 x 5½ in. (56 x 14 cm)—cut 2

Sides: 19¼ x 5½ in. (49 x 14 cm)—cut 2 (one side is reserved for the door)

Bottom roof: 5 x 5½ in. (13 x 14 cm)—cut 2

Top roof: 5¾ x 5½ in. (14.5 x 14 cm)—cut 2

Floor: 4¼ x 5½ in. (11 x 14 cm)—cut 2

Awning for lower storey: 5 x 5½ in. (12.5 x 14 cm)—cut 1

1 Referring to the Basic Birdhouse on page 8, cut and shape the birdhouse pieces from dog-ear fence board, reserving the cut-off pieces for the roof and decorative triangles. Bevel one short end of the awning at 45°, then cut it in half lengthwise. Using a speed square, mark the inside of the front and back panels 10 in. (25 cm) up from the bottom, to show where the divider will be attached. Cut a 1¼-in. (32-mm) entrance hole, 8½ in. (21.5 cm) from the bottom of the front panel and another hole 3½ in. (9 cm) from the peak point, both centered on the width.

2 Assemble the body of the birdhouse, following steps 2–3 of the Basic Birdhouse on page 9. (Do not attach the door just yet.)

3 Using the guide marks that you made in step 1, glue and nail the second floor panel in place as the divider between the two storeys. Attach the door and the roof (see steps 4–7 of the Basic Birdhouse on pages 9–10).

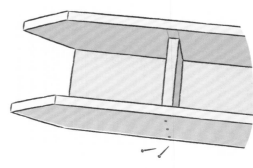

Purple Martin

4 Using a ⁵⁄₁₆-in. (8-mm) bit, drill three holes in a diagonal line under each entrance hole. Insert the dowel perches, with the longer dowels in the top hole on each storey.

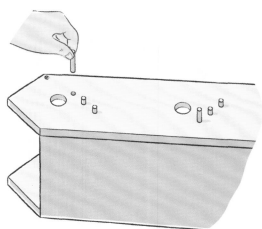

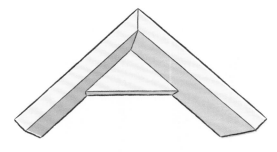

5 Glue and nail the two pieces of the awning together along the beveled edge. Glue and nail a triangular scrap under the apex; you will use this to attach the awning to the birdhouse.

6 Using a speed square, draw a line across the front of the birdhouse, 1½ in. (4 cm) above the lower entrance hole. Apply glue to the back of the awning, taking care not to glue the overhang. Center the base of the awning triangle on your guide line. Nail in three places to secure.

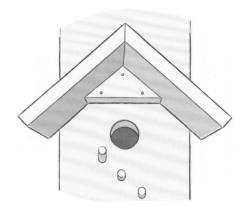

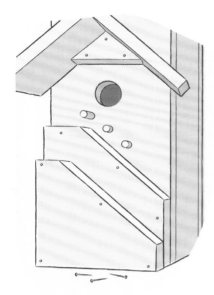

7 Cut two pieces 6¾ in. (17 cm) high out of fence material. Then cut from the top left corner to the right-hand side of each piece at 45°. Cut 1¾ in. (4.5 cm) off the top end and 2¾ in. (7 cm) off the bottom, making two five-sided pieces. Cut another 1½ in. (4 cm) off the bottom of one piece. This will create two steps for the front façade. Glue and nail the step facades together, then glue and nail them to the base of the birdhouse.

8 Glue and nail the triangles that you cut off in the previous step above the awning, overlapping them so that they are both the same distance from the edges of the front of the birdhouse.

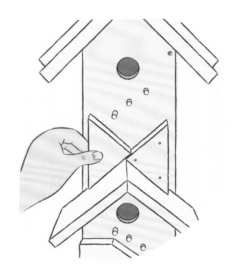

9 Using a speed square and a ⅛-in. (3-mm) bit, mark and drill two pilot holes in the back mount panel, 1½ in. (4 cm) from each side and 1½ in. (4 cm) from the top (see page 136), so that you can attach it to a tree or fence with 2-in. (50-mm) exterior screws. Drill five pilot holes through the back of the birdhouse and the back mount panel and insert 1¼-in. (30-mm) screws. Cut the shaped top off the two 5½-in. (14-cm) dog-ear fence panels and use them for the door knobs.

10 Prepare the birdhouse for painting (see page 10), then prime with brown paint. Paint the roof and awning with hammered copper paint and leave to dry. Mask the roof and awning, then paint the body of the birdhouse navy blue. When dry, apply a final coat of ivory; some of the underlying blue will show through, creating a weathered effect.

11 Paint the "steps," decorative triangles, knobs, and dowel perches bright yellow. Apply dry brush strokes of yellow on the same pieces to make them look darker in spots and dry brush strokes of antique gold metallic paint onto both roofs; when dry, apply strokes of hunter green to the roofs and the edges of the yellow parts. Leave to dry.

12 Varnish the birdhouse and back mount panel (see page 132).

chapter 3

upcycled birdhouses

We all have drawers and sheds that need to be cleaned out from
time to time. From wine corks and broken bits of chain to recycled
spindles, this chapter is packed with ideas for transforming left-over
scraps and bits of junk into something that has real style.

This birdhouse stands on a 24-inch (60-cm) high pedestal made from a recycled spindle. It is intended for use in a garden with a covered porch or patio and will look great between potted plants that flower throughout spring and summer. When birds feel comfortable with humans around, they will nest just about anywhere they like.

pedestal
birdhouse

Eurasian Nuthatch

materials

6 ft x 5½ in. x ½ in. (180 x 14 x 1.2 cm) dog-ear fence board

25 x 4 x 1-in. (64 x 10 x 2.5 cm) hardwood lumber (timber)

24 x 1½ x 1½-in. (60 x 4 x 4-cm) recycled spindle (or buy new from home improvement store)

Waterproof glue

1-in. (25-mm) finish nails or galvanized wire nails

18 x 1¼-in. (30-mm) exterior screws

1 x 2-in. (50-mm) exterior screw

10-in. (25-cm) length of round dowel, ⅜ in. (1 cm) in diameter, for roof and perch

¾-in. (20-mm) wire brads

1-in. (2.5-cm) wire nails

Paintable wood-filler putty

80-grit sandpaper

White primer, soft yellow, and soft blue oil-based exterior spray paints

Red, brown, dark brown, metallic green, and bright yellow exterior craft paints

Waterproof silicone adhesive (30 minutes)

Three round balls, 1 in. (2.5 cm) in diameter, for eggs (optional)

Moss

Water-based exterior varnish

Basic tool kit (see page 132)

finished size

Approx. 37½ x 5½ x 6¾ in. (95 x 14 x 17 cm)

interior dimensions

Floor area: 4¼ x 5½ in. (10.5 x 14 cm)

Cavity depth: 8 in. (20 cm)

Entrance hole to floor: 6 in. (15 cm)

Entrance hole: 1½ in. (40 mm) in diameter

cutting list

N.B. Start your cuts at the straight end of the dog-ear fence panel. You will need the dog-ear end for the birdhouse base panel.

Pedestal foot: 4 x 5½ in. (10 x 14 cm)— cut 4 from hardwood lumber (timber)

Pedestal top: 7 x 5½ in. (18 x 14 cm)— cut one from straight end of dog-ear fence panel

Birdhouse base panel: 9¾ x 5½ in. (24.5 x 14 cm)—cut one from dog-ear end of fence panel

Front and back: 9¼ x 5½ in. (23.5 x 14 cm)—cut 2 from dog-ear fence panel

Sides: 8 x 5½ in. (20 x 14 cm)—cut 2 from dog-ear fence panel (one side is reserved for the door)

Roof: 8½ x 5½ in. (21.5 x 14 cm)—cut 2 from dog-ear fence panel

Floor: 4¼ x 5½ in. (11 x 14 cm)—cut 1 from dog-ear fence panel

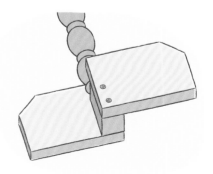

1 From hardwood lumber, cut four 4 x 5½-in. (10 x 14-cm) rectangles for the pedestal feet. On each piece, cut off a corner at one short end at a 45° angle, as shown. Using a ⅛-in. (3-mm) bit, drill two pilot holes (see page 136) about 1 in. (2.5 cm) apart on each side of the spindle base. Apply waterproof glue to the spindle. With the mitered end at the top, aligning the uncut end of the foot with the edge of the first side of the spindle, drive in 1¼-in. (30-mm) screws through the foot sides and into the spindle. Repeat with the other pedestal feet.

2 Using a ⅛-in. (3-mm) bit, drill a pilot hole in the center of the pedestal top. Apply waterproof glue to the top of the spindle. Place the pedestal top over the spindle and drive in a 2-in. (50-m) exterior screw. Insert nails around the screw to secure the top to the spindle and prevent it from spinning around. Once the glue has dried, it will form a tight bond.

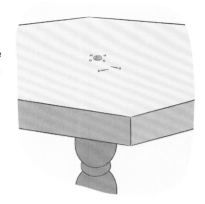

3 Prime the pedestal with white oil-based exterior spray primer and let dry. Paint the pedestal with soft yellow oil-based exterior spray paint and let dry.

4 Referring to the Basic Birdhouse on page 8, cut the birdhouse pieces from dog-ear fence panel. (Start your cuts at the straight end of the fence panel. You will need the dog-ear end for the base of the birdhouse.) Shape the peaks of the front and back panels at a 22.5° angle, reserving the off-cuts. Do not cut the corners off the floor panel. Cut a 1½-in. (40-mm) entrance hole in the front panel, positioning it 7 in. (18 cm) from the bottom and centered on the panel width.

5 Assemble the body of the birdhouse, following steps 2–4 of the Basic Birdhouse on page 9. There should be a ³⁄₁₆-in. (2-mm) gap at the tops of the door and side panel for ventilation. Attach the roof, following the instructions for the Simple Roof on page 11, with a 1½-in. (4-cm) overhang at the front and a ¼-in. (6-mm) overhang at the back.

6 Cut a 1¾-in. (4.5-cm) length of ⅜-in. (1-cm) round dowel for the perch. Cut a ⅜-in. (1-cm) hole 1 in. (2.5 cm) below the entrance hole and tap in the perch. Cut the rest of the round dowel to 8¼ in. (21 cm) long and attach it in the gap between the two roof panels (see step 2 of the Simple Roof on page 11), using ¾-in. (20-mm) wire brads.

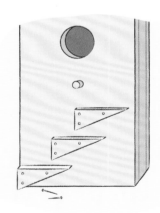

7 Apply waterproof glue to the back of one of the triangular offcuts from the front and back panels. Using a ¹⁄₁₆-in. (1.5-mm) bit, drill three pilot holes. Place the triangle at the base of the front, flush with the left-hand edge, and nail it in place, using 1-in. (25-mm) finish or galvanized wire nails. Repeat with the second and third off-cuts, placing them ½ in. (12 mm) apart and 1½ in. (4 cm) and 2½ in. (6 cm) from the left-hand edge respectively. Attach the fourth off-cut to the door in the same way, positioning it 1¾ in. (4.5 cm) from the left-hand edge and 1¼ in. (3 cm) up from the base of the door.

8 Apply waterproof glue to the edges of the front, side, and back panels of the birdhouse, leaving the door edge free of glue. Using a ⅛-in. (3-mm) bit, drill four pilot holes in the birdhouse base panel. Place the base panel on the birdhouse, extending 2¼ in. (5.5 cm) at the front and ½ in. (12 mm) at the back, with the edges flush with the birdhouse sides. Drill in four 1¼-in. (30-mm) exterior screws to attach the base panel to the birdhouse.

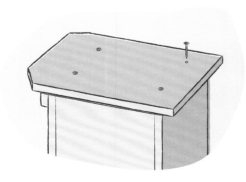

9 Prepare the birdhouse for painting (see step 10 on page 10), then spray with two coats of soft yellow oil-based exterior paint. Let dry.

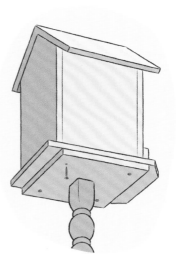

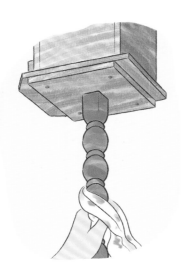

10 Apply waterproof glue to the top of the pedestal, then center the birdhouse base panel on top. Using a ⅛-in. (3-mm) bit, drill four pilot holes in the bottom of the pedestal top. Drill in four 1¼-in. (30-mm) exterior screws to attach the birdhouse to the pedestal.

11 Using a 1-in. (2.5-cm) paint brush swipe red craft paint back and forth over the spindle and birdhouse box, giving a streaked effect. Leave the roof and feet free of red paint. Dilute brown craft paint 1 part paint to 2 parts water. Brush the diluted paint over the spindle only. Wrap a rag around each part of the spindle in turn, then pull it away to create a weathered wood effect.

12 Brush metallic green craft paint sporadically over all four sides of the birdhouse. Using diluted dark brown craft paint (see step 11), brush the diluted paint on one side at a time; while the paint is still wet, dab it with a rag to get the desired effect. Paint the roof, edges of the roof, and underneath the roof in diluted dark brown craft paint, taking care not to let it drip. Do not wipe it off. Leave to dry.

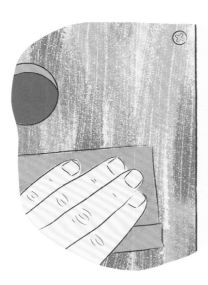

13 Paint the steps, door knob, and one section of the spindle bright yellow. Let dry. Varnish the whole birdhouse and spindle (see page 132). Let dry. Using a circular motion, lightly sand the steps, door knob, spindle, front, sides, back, and base to take off some of the paint and give a weathered look. Varnish once more and let dry.

14 Paint three 1-in. (2.5-cm) balls in a light blue oil-based exterior paint. Let dry. Place waterproof silicone glue on the right-hand side of the porch. Place moss on top and push together to form a round nest, pressing the center in gently to form a hollow for the blue eggs. Place a dab of waterproof silicone glue in the center of the nest and press on the eggs.

15 Place waterproof silicone blue on the top edge of all four feet around the spindle. Press on moss.

I don't know about you, but I save all my wine corks—whether they're from inexpensive wines or top-of–the-range bottles. What a fun conversation piece this would be out on your patio, where friends and family gather to drink wine and eat cheese! Once you open a bottle, simply pop the cork in the birdhouse's entrance hole. When it's full, open the side door and remove the corks to use in your next craft project. And yes—this birdhouse is functional for birds, too!

recycled
wine-cork
birdhouse

materials

Two 6 ft x 5½ in. x ½ in. (180 x 14 x 1.2 cm) dog-ear fence panels

Waterproof glue

1-in. (25-mm) finish nails or galvanized wire nails

Green glass door knob, approx. 1½ in. (4 cm) in diameter

3 x 10-in. (25-cm) lengths of black wire

2 x 1¼-in. (30-mm) exterior screws

1¾-in. (4.5-cm) length of ⁵⁄₁₆-in. (8-mm) round dowel for perch

Paintable wood-filler putty

80-grit sandpaper

Grape-colored oil-based exterior spray paint

Burnt umber and green exterior craft paints

Water-based exterior varnish

8 wine corks

Basic tool kit (see page 132)

finished size

Approx. 14½ x 5½ x 7½ in. (37 x 14 x 19 cm)

interior dimensions

Floor area: 4¼ x 5½ in. (10.75 x 14 cm)
Cavity depth: 11.5 in. (29 cm)
Entrance hole to floor: 8 in. (20 cm)

Entrance hole: 1¼ in. (32 mm) in diameter cutting list

cutting list

Front and back: 12¼ x 5½ in. (31 x 14 cm)—cut 2

Sides: 9½ x 5½ in. (24 x 14 cm)—cut 2 (one side is reserved for the door)

Bottom roof: 5 x 5½ in. (13 x 14 cm)—cut 2

Top roof: 5¾ x 5½ in. (14.5 x 14 cm)—cut 2

Floor: 4¼ x 5½ in. (11 x 14 cm)—cut 1

1 Referring to the Basic Birdhouse on page 8, cut and shape the birdhouse pieces from dog-ear fence board, reserving the cut-off triangular pieces from the front and back panels. Cut a 1¼-in. (32-mm) entrance hole, 8½ in. (21.5 cm) from the bottom of the front panel and centered on the width.

2 Assemble the birdhouse, following steps 2–8 of the Basic Birdhouse on pages 9–10. Attach a 1¾-in. (4.5-cm) length of ⁵⁄₁₆-in. (8-mm) round dowel as a perch (see step 9 on page 10).

3 Glue, then nail three of the reserved triangles to the front of the birdhouse to make shelves for the corks. Attach the last triangle to the peak of the front panel.

4 Prepare the birdhouse for painting (see step 10 on page 10). Paint the sides and base of the birdhouse a purple grape color. Paint the triangles and the trim of the bottom roof panels green.

5 Dilute raw umber craft paint, 1 part paint and 1 part water, for glazing. Starting from the top and leaving the triangles green, paint a small section of the body of the birdhouse at a time, then wipe immediately with a rag or paper towel. Leave to dry.

6 Plug the entrance hole with wadded-up paper or tape, then varnish the birdhouse on all four sides and the base to prevent the glaze from coming off (see page 132). Leave to dry. Then, paint the roof with undiluted raw umber exterior craft paint.

7 Remove the door. Using a 7⁄32-in. (2-mm) bit, drill a hole from the back of the door for the door knob. Attach the door knob, then replace the door.

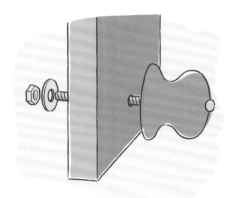

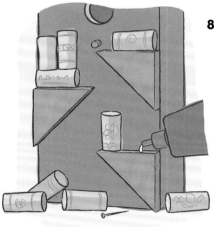

8 Glue and nail on your favorite wine corks where desired.

9 Using 80-grit sandpaper, lightly scuff the edges of the triangles, roof, and birdhouse to create a worn look.

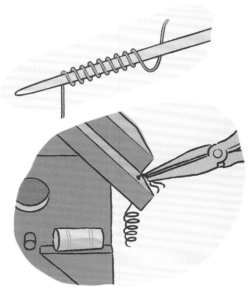

10 Wind the pieces of wire around a pencil or the end of a paintbrush, leaving 2½ in. (6 cm) uncurled. Slip the wire off the pencil. Using a 1⁄16-in. (1.5-mm) bit, drill holes to hang the wire. Push the wires through from under the eaves, then twist the straight ends with pliers to stop them from falling out of the holes.

11 Plug the entrance hole with wadded-up paper or tape, then varnish the exterior of the birdhouse (see page 132).

As the saying goes, "Everyone's trash is someone else's treasure"—and that's what this planter-box birdhouse is all about. I had found an old rusted faucet valve in my garden that I had put away for a rainy day, and gathered other small trinkets from craft stores and our construction business. With this project, anything goes—just use your imagination!

Red-Breasted Nuthatch

planter-box
birdhouse

materials

Two 6 ft x 5½ in. x ½ in. (180 x 14 x 1.2 cm) dog-ear fence panels

Waterproof glue

1-in. (25-mm) finish nails or galvanized wire nails

25–30 x 1¼-in. (30-mm) exterior screws

1¾-in. (4.5-cm) length of ⁵⁄₁₆-in. (8-mm) round dowel for perch

Paintable wood-filler putty

80-grit sandpaper

Black oil-based exterior spray paint

Mid-green oil-based exterior spray paint

Decorative items of your choice—for example, pine bark for the roof, an old fork for the door pull, driftwood sticks, moss, hooks and door plates from your local hardware or craft store, an old rusty faucet (tap), decorative buttons

Multi-purpose waterproof adhesive and small screws to attach the decorations

Cream exterior craft paint

Water-based exterior varnish

Basic tool kit (see page 132)

finished size

Birdhouse: 21½ x 6⅜ x 5½ in. (54.5 x 16.25 x 14 cm)

Planter box: 9 x 22½ in. (23 x 57 cm)

interior dimensions

Floor area: 4¼ x 5½ in. (11 x 14 cm)

Cavity depth: 10 in. (25 cm)

Entrance hole to floor: 8 in. (20 cm)

Entrance hole: 1¼ in. (32 mm)

cutting list

PLANTER BOX

Adapt the measurements to fit your chosen plant containers if necessary.

Base: 21 x 5½ in. (53 x 14 cm)—cut 1

Side panels: 21 x 5½ in. (53 x 14 cm)—cut 2

End panels: 5½ x 5½ in. (14 x 14 cm)—cut 2

BIRDHOUSE

Front: 18 x 5½ in. (45.75 x 14 cm)—cut 1

Back: 13¼ x 5½ in. (33.5 x 14 cm)—cut 1

Sides: 10½ x 5½ in. (26.5 x 14 cm)—cut 2 (one side is reserved for the door)

Bottom roof: 5 x 5½ in. (20 x 14 cm)—cut 2

Top roof: 5¾ x 5½ in. (14.5 x 14 cm)—cut 2

Floor: 4¼ x 5½ in. (11 x 14 cm)—cut 1

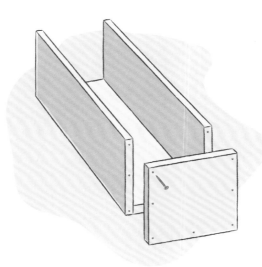

1 Glue and nail the side panels of the planter box to the outside of the base panel, then drill pilot holes (see page 136) and insert 1¼-in. (30-mm) screws for extra security. Attach the end panels to the outside of the side panels in the same way. Drill ⁵⁄₁₆ in. (8-mm) drainage holes in the bottom of the planter box.

2 Paint the inside of the box in black oil-based exterior paint and leave to dry.

3 Referring to the Basic Birdhouse on page 8, cut and shape the birdhouse pieces from dog-ear fence board. To determine where the entrance hole will go, place the front panel on the front of the planter box. Using a speed square, mark a line on the back of the front panel, level with the top edge of the planter box. Cut a 1¼-in. (32-mm) entrance hole, 8½ in. (21.5 cm) above the pencil line and centered on the width.

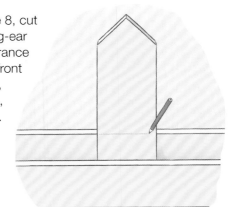

4 Assemble the birdhouse and drill a hole for the dowel perch, following steps 1–9 of the Basic Birdhouse on pages 9–10, aligning the front, side and back panels at the top; the front panel will overhang the others at the base, so that you can attach it to the planter box.

5 Prepare the planter box and birdhouse for painting (see step 10 on page 10). Turn the planter box upside down to avoid getting paint on the inside, then paint the planter box and birdhouse mid-green.

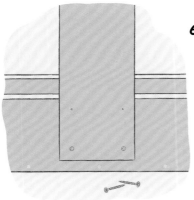

6 Using a ⅛-in. (3-mm) bit, drill four pilot holes (see page 136) at the base of the front panel, then insert 1¼-in. (30-mm) screws to attach the birdhouse to the front of the planter box.

7 Attach your chosen embellishments wherever you choose. You can give metal items, such as door plates and hooks, the patina of old bronze by lightly dabbing on two shades of green craft paint.

8 Dry brush the outside of the birdhouse and planter box with cream exterior craft paint, allowing some of the underlying green to show through (wipe off excess paint with a rag if necessary). Varnish the outside of the birdhouse (see page 132).

9 Place the planter on a shelf or attach it to a 4 x 4-in. (10 x 10-cm) post, screwing decorative corbels to the plant base and the sides of the post.

It's always great to find a use for all those objects that you just couldn't bear to throw away. On this unusually shaped birdhouse, I used S-hooks, metal screws, composite shims, a screwdriver that came with a kit of some sort, and metal roof flashing. You could omit the embellishments and hang the birdhouse from a pipe clamp (clip) if you prefer. There is an opening on the bottom that the hub connector will cover for cleaning out.

pyramid **birdhouse**

materials

One 6 ft x 5½ in. x ½ in. (180 x 14 x 1.2 cm) dog-ear fence panel

Waterproof glue

7-in. (18-cm) length of 1 x 1-in. (2.5 x 2.5-cm) lumber (timber)

1-in. (25-mm) finish nails or galvanized wire nails

Paintable wood-filler putty

80-grit sandpaper

Purple oil-based exterior spray paint

Water-based exterior varnish

8 x 1½-in. (38-mm) S-hooks

9 x ⅝-in. (15-mm) metal screws

3 packs composite shims

¾-in. (20-mm) wire nails (for composite shim attachment)

5 x 7-in. (12.5 x 18-cm) roof flashing tile

10 x ¾-in. (20-mm) wood screws (for metal roof)

Metal screwdriver, key, or 1¾-in. (4.5-cm) length of ⁵⁄₁₆-in. (8-mm) round dowel, for perch

1-in. (2.5-cm) HS hub connector (from electrical section of home store)

4 x 1¼-in. (30-mm) exterior screws for hub connector

4 x ¼-in. (6-mm) nuts

1 x 6-in. (2.5 x 15-cm) galvanized nipple

6-ft (1.8-m) hollow galvanized fence pipe

Two 4-foot (1.2-m) rebars (reinforcing bars), ⁵⁄₁₆ in. (8 mm) in diameter

Basic tool kit (see page 132)

finished size

7½ x 15 x 5½ in. (19 x 38 x 14 cm)

interior dimensions

Floor area: 4¼ x 10 in. (11 x 25 cm)
Cavity depth: 5 in. (12.5 cm)
Entrance hole to floor: 4 in. (10 cm)
Entrance hole: 1 in. (25 mm) in diameter

cutting list

Front and back: 7⅝ x 7⅝ x 10¾ in. (18.5 x 18.5 x 27.3 cm)—cut 2
Roof: 9 x 5½ in. (23 x 14 cm)—cut 2
Bottom panel: 12¼ x 5½ in. (31 x 14 cm)—cut 1

1 Cut two triangle shapes for the front and back panels, cutting across the straight end of a dog-ear fence panel at a 45° angle, as shown. Cut a 1-in. (2.5-cm) entrance hole in the front panel 1½ in. (4 cm) from the peak and centered on the width.

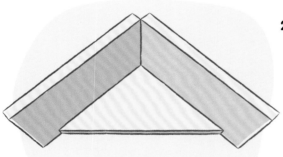

2 Glue and nail the two roof panels flush to the edge of the back panel on each side, then glue and nail the front panel flush to the edges of the roof panels on each side, leaving a V-shaped gap along the ridge of the roof.

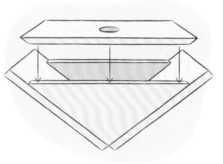

3 Bevel each short end of the bottom panel at 45°. Cut a 2½-in. (6.5-cm) hole in the center of the bottom panel for cleaning out the birdhouse when necessary. Glue and nail the bottom panel to the front, back, and roof sides.

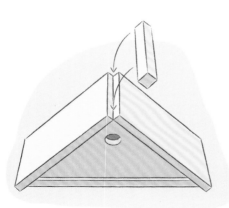

4 Glue and nail a 7-in. (18-cm) length of 1 x 1-in. (2.5 x 2.5-cm) square lumber to the V-shaped gap in the ridge of the roof, with the end flush with the back panel and the tip overhanging at the front. (Nail the piece at a slight angle to ensure proper attachment.)

5 Prepare the birdhouse for painting (see step 10 on page 10), then spray with purple oil-based exterior paint.

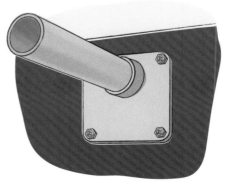

6 Center the hub connector hole over the clean-out hole in the base. Using a ⅛-in. (3-mm) bit, drill a pilot hole in the center of each hole of the hub connector. Drill in 1¼-in. (30-mm) exterior screws with ¼-in. (6-mm) nut on the neck of each screw to prevent sharp tip from penetrating through to the floor bottom. Screw the 6-in. (15-cm) length of nipple to the hub connector.

7 Measure the composite shims against the roof and cut them to size, using utility scissors. Each row will hold four shims, with a slight overhang at the sides and at the bottom. Starting in the center of the roof and working outward, glue and nail the first row in place, using ¾-in. (20-mm) nails. Attach three more rows in the same way, starting each row 1½ in. (4 cm) higher up than the previous one. The top row should end level with the base of the square roof ridge.

8 For the perch, I used a screwdriver that came with a self-assembly shelf kit; I simply drilled a hole the right size about 1 in. (2.5 cm) below the entrance hole and hammered the screwdriver in place. (Alternatively, you could use a 1¾-in. (4.5-cm) length of round dowel.) Drill a pilot hole in the square end of the front roof ridge, place a machine nut over the hole, and drive in a 1½-in. (40-mm) screw.

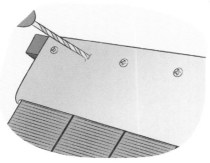

9 Remove the sharp edges from the roof flashing tile by curling the corners inward with a pair of needle-nose pliers. Bend the flashing tile in half over the roof ridge. Mark where each screw needs to go with a black marker pen. Using a ⅟₁₆-in. (1.5-mm) bit, drill pilot holes through the metal 1½ in. (4 cm) apart, starting ½ in. (12 mm) from the front end of the roof ridge and ¾ in. (2 cm) down from the top of the metal. Change to a ⅛-in. (3-mm) bit and drill pilot holes at the same points, then screw in ¾-in. (20-mm) wood screws.

10 Starting from the center and working outward, using a ⅛-in. (3-mm) bit or one that is slightly smaller than the screw neck, drill a pilot hole for the first screw. Drill the screw in slightly, then place the end of an S-hook under each side and tighten the screw. Repeat all the way across the front panel.

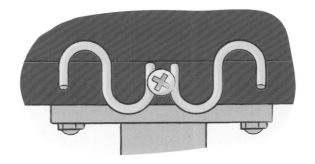

11 Varnish the painted areas of the birdhouse (see page 132). The varnish can go over the screws and S-hooks on the front, but you do not need to varnish the shims.

12 Mount the birdhouse on a hollow galvanized fence pipe, then plant the post in your garden, over 4-foot rebars (see page 137).

With lengths of chain dangling down, this birdhouse reminds me of an old barn with farming equipment attached and reminds me of spending time with my Gramps, rounding up the cattle. I used broken chain from a hanging basket—a great way of recycling junk! A natural knot in the wood provides the entrance hole; knots should be at least 1 to 1½ in. (2.5 to 4 cm) in diameter for birds to be able to enter the box and nest.

Pied Flycatcher

knot-hole birdhouse
with chains

materials

One 6ft x 7½ in. x ½ in. (180 x 19 x 1.2 cm) dark wood dog-ear fence board with knots

One 6ft x 5½ in. x ½ in. (180 x 14 x 1.2 cm) dark wood dog-ear fence board

Waterproof glue

1-in. (25-mm) finish nails or galvanized wire nails

80-grit sandpaper

2 x 1¼-in. (30-mm) exterior screws for door swing

2 x 2½-in. (60-mm) exterior screw

5 x ¾-in. (20-mm) black decorative screws

40 in. (1 m) black small-link chain

Water-based exterior varnish

Basic tool kit (see page 132)

finished size

Approx. 14 x 9 x 9 in. (35.5 x 23 x 23 cm)

interior dimensions

Floor area: 6¼ x 5½ in. (16 x 14 cm)

Cavity depth: 12 in. (30 cm)

Entrance hole to floor: 8 in. (20 cm)

Entrance hole: 1–1½ in. (25–40 mm) in diameter

cutting list

Front and back panels: 13¼ x 7½ in. (33.5 x 19 cm)—cut 2 (one with a knot hole, one without)

Right side panel: 8½ x 5½ in. (21.5 x 14 cm)—cut 1 for door

Left side panel: 13¼ x 5½ in. (33.5 x 14 cm)—cut 1

Floor: 6¼ x 5½ in. (16 x 14 cm)—cut 1

Flat roof: 7½ x 4½ in. (19 x 11.5 cm)—cut 1

Pitched roof: 7 x 7½ in. (17.5 x 19 cm)—cut 1

Door façade: 7 x 3 in. (17.5 x 7.5 cm)—cut 1 with a knot hole in the center

Awning: 2½ x 4½ in. (6.5 x 11.5 cm)—cut 1

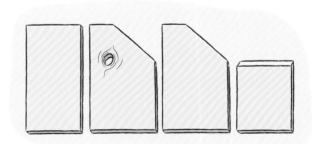

1   In the wood for the front panel, find a knot that's in the right place, slightly off center. Cut the front panel, cutting the base of the panel 8½ in. (21.5 cm) below the knot. Carefully cut out the knot if necessary; ideally, you want a piece of board where the knot has already gone or is loose, so that you don't have to cut it, but this may not be possible. Cut the back panel from a section of the board that does not have a knot. Using a speed square, mark 3 in. (7.5 cm) along the top of the front and back panels and cut from here to the side at a 45° angle. Reserve the off-cuts to use later. Bevel one short edge of the right side panel (the door) at 45°; do not bevel the left side panel.

2 Assemble the body of the birdhouse, following steps 2–4 of the Basic Birdhouse on page 9.

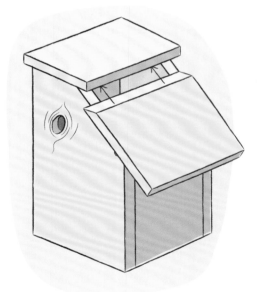

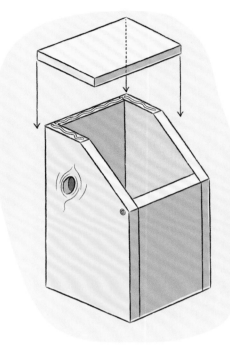

3 Glue and nail the flat roof in place, flush with the edge of the back and left side panels and overhanging the door by 1½ in. (4 cm) and the front panel by ½ in. (1 cm).

4 Bevel one short end of the pitched roof panel at 45°. Glue and nail the pitched roof panel under the flat roof, with the beveled edge uppermost.

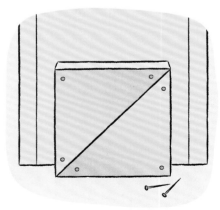

5 Place the off-cuts from the front and back panels together to form a square. Glue and nail them to the door to form the door pull. If you wish, drill in 1¼-in. (30-mm) screws from the inside of the door through to the door pull, for extra strength.

6 Remove the door. Using a ⅛-in. (3-mm) bit, drill pilot holes in the panel opposite the door, then drill in 2½-in. (60-mm) exterior screws so that you can mount the birdhouse on a tree or fence post.

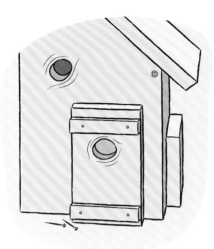

7 Cut a ¼-in. (6-mm) sliver off each short end of the door façade. Glue and nail the door façade to the front of the birdhouse, 1 in. (2.5 cm) from the right-hand side and flush with the bottom. Using a ¹⁄₁₆-in. (1.5-mm) bit, drill a tiny hole in each end of the slivers of wood. Glue one sliver above and one below the knot in the door façade and gently hammer in 1-in. (25-mm) nails to attach.

8 Bevel one long edge of the awning at 45°. Glue and nail it in place on the front panel, above the entrance hole.

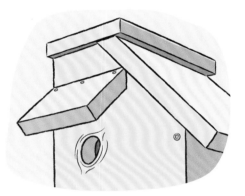

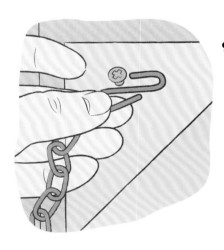

9 Decide where you want to attach the decorative chains. Using a ⅛-in. (3-mm) bit, drill a pilot hole at each attachment point. Drive a ¾-in. (20-mm) decorative black screw partway in at each point, open a chain link, wrap it around the screw, then close the link again. Tighten the screw to hold the chain in place.

10 Protect the entrance hole with wadded-up paper or tape, then varnish the exterior of the birdhouse (see page 132).

11 Drill a ⁵⁄₁₆-in. (8-mm) hole in the center of the floor for drainage. Drill ⁵⁄₁₆-in. (8-mm) ventilation holes in the door, just under the eaves, slanting them slightly upward to prevent rainwater from seeping in.

Upcycling is the process of converting waste materials or useless products into new materials or products of better quality or a higher environmental value. In this birdhouse, I used wine corks from all the vintages of wine that I love. The birdhouse also has a cognac cork for the chimney and a cork for the doorknob.

upcycled wine
cork birdhouse

materials

One 6 ft x 5½ in. x ½ in. (180 x 14 x 1.2 cm) dog-ear fence board

Waterproof glue

1-in. (25-mm) finish nails or galvanized wire nails

½-in. (12-mm) finish nails or galvanized wire nails

5 x 1⅝-in. (40-mm) exterior screws

2 x 1¼-in. (30-mm) exterior screws

Cognac cork for chimney

1 x 1-in. (25-mm) EMT two-hole pipe clamp (clip)

2 x ¾-in. (20-mm) wood screws for pipe clamp (clip)

Paintable wood-filler putty

80-grit sandpaper

Green oil-based exterior spray paint

Brown exterior craft paint

Water-based exterior varnish

Approx. 95 wine corks (some will be cut in half)

Small bunch of artificial grapes

30 in. (75 cm) heavy wire tie

8 sticks, 2–7 in. (5–18 cm) in length

Green moss

Basic tool kit (see page 132)

Finished size

Approx. 12 x 11 x 7 in. (30 x 28 x 18 cm)

Interior dimensions

Floor area: 4¼ x 5½ in. (11 x 14 cm)

Cavity depth: 9 in. (23 cm)

Entrance hole to floor: 6 in. (15 cm)

Entrance hole: 1½ in. (40 mm)

cutting list

Front and back: 9¼ x 5½ in. (23.5 x 14 cm)—cut 2

Sides: 6¼ x 5½ in. (16 x 14 cm)—cut 2 (one side is reserved for the door)

Bottom roof: 5 x 5½ in. (13 x 14 cm)—cut 2

Top roof: 5¾ x 5½ in. (14.5 x 14 cm)—cut 1

Floor: 4¼ x 5½ in. (11 x 14 cm)—cut 1

Porch: 10½ x 5½ in. (26.5 x 14 cm)—cut 1 from dog-ear end of panel

1 Referring to the Basic Birdhouse on page 8, cut and shape the birdhouse pieces from dog-ear fence board. Cut a ½-in. (40-mm) entrance hole, 6½ in. (16.5 cm) from the bottom of the front panel and centered on the width.

2 Assemble the birdhouse, following steps 2–8 of the Basic Birdhouse on pages 9–10.

3 Drill a ⅛-in. (3-mm) pilot hole just below the roof ridge to attach the cork chimney. Drill in a 1⅝-in. (40-mm) exterior screw from the underside of the roof, protruding on the outside of the roof.

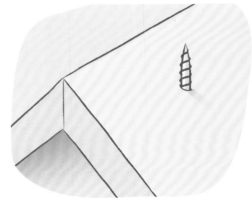

4 Using a hand saw, cut the cork for the chimney at a 45° angle. Apply waterproof glue under and around the cork, then twist it down onto the screw until it is flush with the roof. Wipe off any excess glue.

5 Attach a 1-in. (25-mm) EMT two-hole pipe clamp (clip) to the apex of the roof for a hanging loop (see page 138).

6 Prepare the birdhouse for painting (see step 10 on page 10). Spray the outside of the birdhouse and both sides of the bottom platform with green paint.

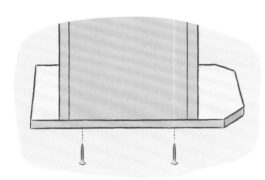

7 Drill ⅛-in. (3-mm) pilot holes through the bottom of the porch, then attach the birdhouse to the porch with 1¼-in. (30-mm) screws, making sure that the back of the porch extends 1½ in. (4 cm) beyond the back panel of the birdhouse. The dog-ear end of the porch should be at the front of the birdhouse.

8 Remove the door of the birdhouse. Drill a ⅛-in. (3-mm) pilot hole from the back of the door, then drill in a 1¼-in. (30-mm) screw. Twist a wine cork onto the screw for the door knob.

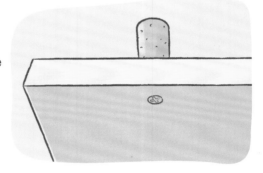

9 Using waterproof glue, start adding full corks to the front of the birdhouse, then nail in place ¼ in. (6 mm) from each end of each cork. Use a hand saw to cut corks at angles or trim them to fit in tight spots. If small bits of cork are protruding or causing an obstruction, trim with utility scissors. Gently hammer cork trimmings into any gaps.

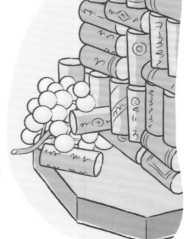

10 Glue a small bunch of artificial grapes to the front porch for extra decoration, adding a cork or two to the porch as well to make a more attractive arrangement.

11 Glue and nail half corks to the door of the birdhouse, making sure you don't nail corks to the side edges of the other panels in order to allow the door to open. Keep checking the door to make sure glue has not seeped between the crack of the door onto the edge or that you've accidentally nailed the door shut. Glue and nail half corks to the side opposite the door.

12 Glue and nail six full corks vertically to the porch on the back of the birdhouse with a seventh cork horizontally on top. Paint the roof with diluted brown exterior craft paint (1 part paint to 3 parts water), to allow the green color to bleed through. Let dry. Varnish the birdhouse (see page 132). Let dry.

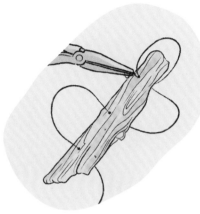

13 Using a ⅛-in. (3-mm) bit, drill three holes through a 6-in. (15-cm) piece of driftwood, in the center of the wood and 1½ in. (4 cm) from each end. Thread wire through the holes, as shown. Loop the hanger end of the wire through the top hole again to create a loop for hanging, then twist with pliers to keep the wire tight and secure.

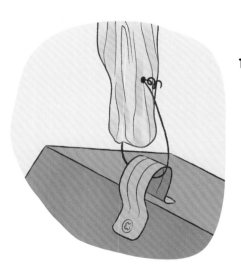

14 Loop the other end of the wire through the pipe clamp (clip), then form into a loop, as in the previous step.

15 Glue green moss to the front porch, tucking it in wherever it looks sparse. Glue moss to the front edge of the roof, and nail driftwood sticks on top. Glue and nail one or two driftwood sticks to the front porch. Using silicone adhesive, glue another stick on top to hid the nail holes.

chapter 4
novelty birdhouses

Once you've conquered the world of woodworking, why not make
a more unusual birdhouse to adorn your garden landscape? Try a
church or a ship, or a house shaped and painted to resemble your
favorite bird—who says birdhouses have to be boring boxes?

A simple birdhouse for small cavity-nesting birds, this birdhouse can easily be hung from an iron garden pole. Although the box seems small, the area in which the birds will build their nest is the perfect size. Ventilation holes on the back and both sides also act as drainage. The side door lifts for easy clean-out, with the screw keeping the door secure while birds are caring for their young.

hanging cube **birdhouse**

materials

One 6 ft x 5½ in. x ½ in. (180 x 14 x 1.2 cm) dog-ear fence panel

Waterproof glue

1-in. (25-mm) finish nails or galvanized wire nails

3 x 1¼-in. (30-mm) exterior screws

80-grit sandpaper

Paintable wood-filler putty

1¾-in. (4.5-cm) length of round dowel, ⁵⁄₁₆ in. (8 mm) in diameter, for perch

Lime-green oil-based exterior spray paint

Dark brown and dark green exterior craft paint

Water-based exterior varnish

2 x large chain links

1 x 5-in. (12-cm) length of chain

1 x 1-in. (25-mm) EMT two-hole pipe clamp (clip)

2 x ¾-in. (20-mm) wood screws

Basic tool kit (see page 132)

finished size

Approx. 10¾ x 8¾ x 5½ in. (27.5 x 22.25 x 14 cm)

interior dimensions

Floor area: 6 x 4 in. (15 x 10 cm)

Cavity depth: 6 in. (15 cm)

Entrance hole to floor: 4 in. (10 cm)

Entrance hole: 1¼ in. (32 mm) in diameter

cutting list

Front and back: 5½ x 5½ in. (14 x 14 cm)—cut 2

Roof panel 1: 5½ x 7½ in. (14 x 19 cm)—cut 1

Roof panel 2: 5½ x 7¾ in. (14 x 19.5 cm)—cut 1

Left side panel: 4¾ x 4 in. (12 x 10 cm)—cut 1

Right side panel (door): 5¼ x 4 in. (13.25 x 10 cm)—cut 1

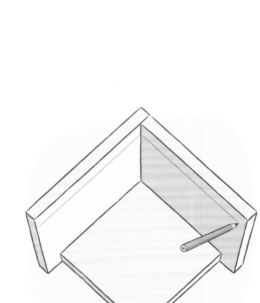

Great Tit

1 Cut the birdhouse pieces from dog-ear fence panel. Turn the front panel so that you're looking at it as a diamond shape. Cut a 1¼-in. (32-mm) entrance hole, 1¾ in. (32 mm) from the top point and centered on the width.

2 Glue and nail the long roof panel over the top of the short roof panel. Glue and nail the back panel flush to the inside edge of the roof panels, nailing from the top of the roof panels. At each corner where the back panel meets the roof panel, measure 4 in. (10 cm) up the roof panel and make a pencil mark to show where the front panel will attach to the underside of the roof.

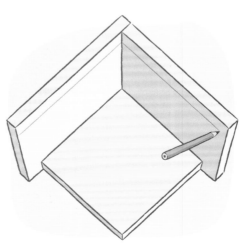

3 Glue and nail the front panel in place, nailing from the top of the roof panels. The roof will slightly overhang the front of the birdhouse.

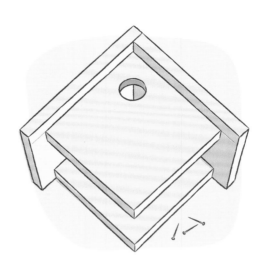

4 Glue and nail the left side panel to the inside edges of the front and back panels. Using a ⅛-in. (3-mm) bit, drill pilot holes (see page 136) on the sides of the front and back panels, then attach the right side panel (the door) using 1¼-in. (30-mm) exterior screws. As this door is on a downward slope, you will also need to drill another pilot hole from the base of the right-side panel and screw in a 1¼-in. (30-mm) exterior screw so that the door can't open during the nesting season; slightly unscrew this screw to remove the nest when necessary.

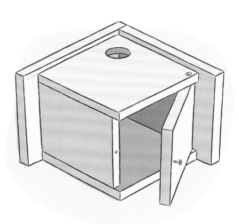

5 Drill a hole in the front panel about 1 in. (2.5 cm) below the entrance hole and gently tap in the round dowel for the perch (see step 9 on page 10). Using a ³⁄₁₆-in. (5-mm) bit, drill holes just under the eaves on both sides and the back panel for ventilation and drainage, sloping upward to prevent water from dripping in.

6 Prepare the birdhouse for painting (see step 10 on page 10). Prime with gray oil-based exterior spray paint. Leave to dry, then paint with lime-green oil-based exterior spray paint. Leave to dry.

7 Apply dark brown exterior craft paint to the roof. While still slightly damp, apply dark green in uneven strips. Leave to dry. Varnish the exterior of the birdhouse (see page 132).

8 Attach a large chain link to each end of a 5-in. (12.5-cm) length of chain. (Alternatively, ask your local home-improvement store to make a chain-link hanger.) Thread one chain link through a 1-in. (2.5-cm) pipe clamp (clip), then attach the clamp to the top of the birdhouse, following the instructions on page 138.

9 If you wish, paint the pipe clamp with dark brown exterior craft paint and let dry.

This is a fun project for the whole family to get involved in, and it will teach children all about the birds in the garden. What child wouldn't want to help make something pretty for birds to nest in and rear their young?

flower and ladybug **birdhouse**

materials

One 6 ft x 5½ in. x ½ in. (180 x 14 x 1.2 cm) dog-ear fence panel

Waterproof glue

1-in. (25-mm) finish nails or galvanized wire nails

2 x 1¼-in. (30-mm) exterior screws

1 x 1-in. (25-mm) EMT two-hole pipe clamp (clip)

2 x ¾-in. (20-mm) wood screws for pipe clamp (clip)

Paintable wood-filler putty

80-grit sandpaper

Gray exterior wood primer paint

Pink oil-based exterior spray paint

Dark blue, bright blue, ivy, light green, dark green, lemon, black, and dark brown exterior craft paints

Ladybug stick pins

Glass door knob or drawer knob, approx. 1–1½ in. (2.5–4 cm) in diameter

1¾-in. (4.5-cm) length of round dowel, ⁵⁄₁₆ in. (8 mm) in diameter, for perch

Water-based exterior varnish

Basic tool kit (see page 132)

finished size

Approx. 11 x 6¾ x 5½ in. (28 x 17 x 14 cm)

interior dimensions

Floor area: 4¼ x 5½ in. (10.75 x 14 cm)
Cavity depth: 8 in. (20 cm)
Entrance hole to floor: 6 in. (15 cm)
Entrance hole: 1¼ in. (32 mm)

cutting list

Front and back: 9 x 5½ in. (23 x 14 cm)—cut 2

Sides: 6¼ x 5½ in. (16 x 14 cm)—cut 2 (one side is reserved for the door)

Bottom roof: 5 x 5½ in. (20 x 14 cm)—cut 2

Top roof: 5¾ x 5½ in. (14.5 x 14 cm)—cut 2

Floor: 4¼ x 5½ in. (11 x 14 cm)—cut 1

1 Referring to the Basic Birdhouse on page 8, cut and shape the birdhouse pieces from dog-ear fence board. Cut a 1¼-in. (32-mm) entrance hole, 6½ in. (16.5 cm) from the bottom of the front panel and centered on the width.

2 Assemble the birdhouse and prepare it for painting, following steps 2–8 of the Basic Birdhouse on pages 9–10.

3 Attach a 1-in. (25-mm) EMT two-hole pipe clamp (clip) to the apex of the roof for a hanging loop (see page 138).

4 Prime the birdhouse (including the base) with gray exterior primer paint. Leave to dry. Go over the primer with any color of exterior paint you choose; I used bright pink. Don't worry if some of the primer color shows through a little in places—it looks cool and gives the birdhouse a slightly worn, weathered look. Paint the roof in dark brown exterior craft paint.

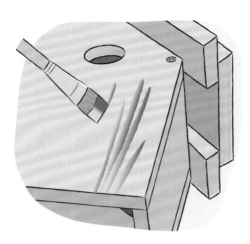

5 The painting technique used here uses two colors at a time on the same brush—dip half of the tip in one color and the other half in the second color. (Practice on white paper first.) First, use a ¾-in. (2-cm) brush and bright green and light green paint to make long stems around the base of the birdhouse. Then repeat the process, using a ½-in. (12-mm) brush and lemon yellow and light green paint, making fewer strokes this time. Finally, using a long, thin brush, paint longer lines in dark green and lemon yellow, making an odd number of strokes on each birdhouse panel.

6 Now load a ½-in. (12-mm) brush with blue paint—dark blue on the front of the tip and light blue on the back. Press the dark blue end down first, then lift and make a circle of petals with an empty spot in the center. Make 3–5 flowers on each side.

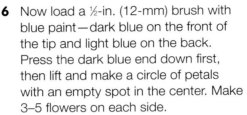

7 Using a small, thin brush, fill in the flower centers with black paint. While it is still wet, pull lines of paint outward all around to create spiderlike centers. With a long slim brush, paint lemon yellow stripes all around the petals to give them more depth.

8 Using a ¹⁄₁₆-in. (1.5-mm) pin bit, drill a small pilot hole for the ladybug pins. With a ⁵⁄₁₆-in. (8-mm) bit, make a small indention around the pin holes. Apply waterproof glue to the holes and place the pins in position. Using a a finish hammer, gently tap the pins into the wood. Attach 3–5 ladybugs to the front panel; add more to the other panels if you wish.

9 Using a ³⁄₁₆-in. (5-mm) bit, drill a hole from the back of the door and attach the door knob. I offset the door knob to make it a little more interesting.

10 Drill a hole for the dowel perch and insert the perch into the hole (see step 9 on page 10). Paint the perch to match the flowers. Varnish the exterior of the birdhouse (see page 132).

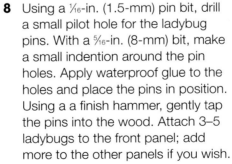

An attractive novelty birdhouse that can be painted to look like your favorite bird, this sits high on galvanized fence posting and has ventilation holes on the back end and the front, just under the beak.

bird's eye **birdhouse**

Eastern Bluebird

materials

One 6 ft x 7½ in. x 2½ in. (180 x 19 x 1.2 cm) dog-ear fence board

One 6 ft x 5½ in. x 2½ in. (180 x 14 x 1.2 cm) dog-ear fence board

10 x 4 x ½ in. (25 x 10 x 1.2 cm) lumber (timber) for wing

1¾-in. (4.5-cm) length of ⁵⁄₁₆-in. (8-mm) round dowel for perch

80-grit sandpaper

Waterproof glue

1-in. (25-mm) finish nails or galvanized wire nails

Medium blue oil-based exterior spray paint

Orange, light blue, light grey, and black exterior craft paint

9 x 1¼-in. (30-mm) exterior screws

Water-based exterior varnish

Galvanized hollow steel fence post

4 x ¼-in. (6-mm) nuts

1-in. (2.5-cm) HS hub connector (from electrical section of home store)

1 x 6-in. (2.5 x 15-cm) galvanized nipple

4 x 1⅝-in. (40-mm) exterior screws

Two 4-foot (1.2-m) rebar (reinforcing bars), ½ in. (12 mm) in diameter

Basic tool kit (see page 132)

finished size

Approx. 10 x 20 x 7¾ in. (25 x 50 x 19.5 cm)

interior dimensions

Floor area: 13 x 5½ in. (33 x 14 cm)

Cavity depth: 6¾ in. (17 cm)

Entrance hole to floor: 6 in. (15 cm)

Entrance hole: 1½ in. (40 mm) in diameter

cutting list

Front and back: 14 x 2¾ x 8 x 2¾ x 10¾ in. (35.5 x 7 x 20 x 7 x 27.3 cm)—cut 2 from 7½-in. (19-cm) fence board (see step 1)

Top panel: 13 x 5½ in. (33 x 14 cm)—cut 1 from straight end of 5½-in. (14-cm) fence board

Beak: 3½ x 5½ in. (9 x 14 cm)—cut 1 from dog-ear end of 5½-in. (14-cm) fence board

Butt: 9¾ x 5½ in. (24.7 x 14 cm)—cut 1 from 5½-in. (14-cm) fence board

Floor panel: 2½ x 5½ in. (6.3 x 14 cm)—cut 1 from 5½-in. (14-cm) fence board

Breast panel: 7¼ x 5½ in. (18.5 cm)—cut 1 from 5½-in. (14-cm) fence board

Base panel: 6 x 5½ in. (15 x 14 cm)—cut 1 from 7½-in. (19-cm) fence board

Roof panel 1: 16 x 7½ in. (40.5 x 19 cm)—cut 1 from straight end of 7½-in. (19-cm) fence board

Roof panel 2: 5 x 7½ in. (12.5 x 19 cm)—cut 1 from dog-ear end of 7½-in. (19-cm) fence board

Wing: 10 x 4 in. (25 x 10 cm)—cut 1 from lumber (timber)

1 Cut the front panel from the dog-ear end of 7½-in. (19-cm) fence board. This may look complicated, but you simply measure 14 in. (35.5 cm) along one edge from the base of the dog ear and make a straight cut across the board, and then make a 45° cut on each end of the board, as shown in the diagram. Then place the front panel on the remaining board and draw around it, and cut out the back panel; this way, the two panels are identical.

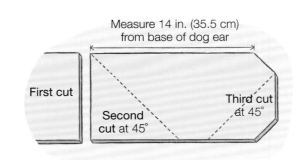

Measure 14 in. (35.5 cm) from base of dog ear

First cut

Second cut at 45°

Third cut at 45°

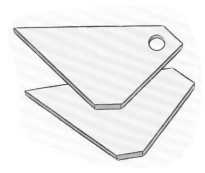

2 Cut a 1½-in. (40-mm) entrance hole in the front panel 1½ in. (4 cm) down from the top edge and 1½ in. (4 cm) from the point.

3 Bevel one short side of the top panel at 45° and the other short side at 22.5°. Glue and nail the front panel to the top panel edge, with the 22.5° bevel of the top panel at the entrance-hole end and the 45° bevel at the tail end. Glue and nail the back panel to the top panel in the same way. Bevel one long side of the beak at 22.5°, then glue and nail the beveled end of the beak to the end of the top panel.

4 Bevel one short side of the butt at 45° and the other at 22.5°. Glue and nail the sides and 45° beveled end of the butt to the other end of the top panel, leaving the 22.5° end of the butt without glue.

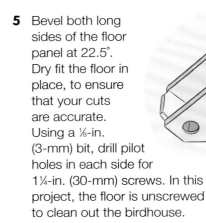

5 Bevel both long sides of the floor panel at 22.5°. Dry fit the floor in place, to ensure that your cuts are accurate. Using a ⅛-in. (3-mm) bit, drill pilot holes in each side for 1¼-in. (30-mm) screws. In this project, the floor is unscrewed to clean out the birdhouse.

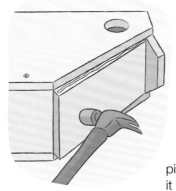

6 Bevel one short side of the breast panel at 22.5°. Glue and nail the straight-cut end and the sides of the breast in place, leaving the beveled end free of glue. You may have to tap the piece gently with a hammer to fit it in place.

7 Using a ³⁄₁₆-in. (5-mm) bit, drill four holes for drainage in the floor. Using the pilot holes that you drilled in step 5, drill in 1¼-in. (30-mm) screws to attach the floor panel between the breast and butt panels.

8 Using a ⁵⁄₁₆-in. (8-mm) bit, drill ventilation holes at a downward angle on the butt and breast panels.

9 Using a ⅛-in. (3-mm) bit, drill a pilot hole for a 1¼-in. (30-mm) screw in the middle of the base panel. This will be where the hub connector is attached once the birdhouse is complete.

10 On roof panel 1, bevel one short end at 22.5°. On roof panel 2, bevel the end opposite the dog ear at 22.5°. Cut the un-beveled short end of roof panel 1 at 45° on each side, leaving 1½ in. (4 cm) straight cut in the center. Glue and nail roof panels 1 and 2 to the top panel along their beveled edges, positioning them flush with the back panel and overhanging the front by 2 in. (5 cm). This will provide an awning to protect the entrance hole.

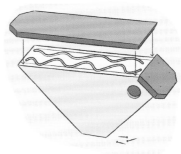

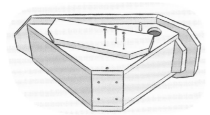

11 Make a 45° miter cut 1½ in. (4 cm) from the each edge on the bottom of the wing. Using a ⅛-in. (3-mm) bit, drill three pilot holes as shown. Glue the wing in place on the front of the bird, then drill in 1¼-in. (30-mm) exterior screws. Using a ⁵⁄₁₆-in. (8-mm) bit, drill a hole for the dowel perch (see step 9 on page 10) and insert the perch.

12 Prepare the birdhouse for painting (see step 10 on page 10), then paint it bright blue. Paint the base panel, too.

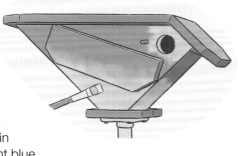

13 When the paint is dry, attach the base panel to the bottom of the birdhouse with a 1¼-in. (30-mm) screw. Drill in two more screws, one on either side of the central one. Attach a 1-in (2.5-cm) hub connector to the bottom of the floor, with the hole centered over the painted blue screw, using four ¼-in. (6-mm) nuts to ensure that the screws do not protrude through to the inside of birdhouse. Attach the nipple pipe.

14 Prepare the birdhouse for painting (see step 10 on page 10). I used colors similar to those on an Eastern Bluebird, applying orange exterior craft paint to the side, breast, butt, and around the eye area, and then blended in touches of light grey and light blue here and there.

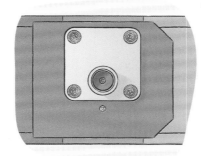

15 Then I added black around the eye area, painted the beak solid black, and dry brushed black streaks around the bottom of the wing. If you wish, you can paint the back panel in the same way. Leave to dry, then varnish the birdhouse (see page 132).

16 Mount the birdhouse on a hollow galvanized fence pipe, then plant the post in your garden over 4-ft rebars (see page 137).

With its large entrance hole and spacious interior, this birdhouse is designed to impress! Old spindles are used to create ancient pillars on the front porch, where steps lead up to a grand entrance. This birdhouse can perch on a post or sit on a shelf as a decorative piece for any birdhouse collector.

church **birdhouse**

materials

Two 6 ft x 7½ in. x ½ in. (180 x 19 x 1.2 cm) dog-ear fence boards

Waterproof glue

1-in. (25-mm) finish nails or galvanized wire nails

10 x 1¼-in. (30-mm) exterior screws

Two recycled spindles for pillars (or purchase at home store)

3-ft (90-cm) length of 2 x 2-in. (5 x 5-cm) square spindle for steeple

2 x 1⅝-in. (40-mm) exterior screws

80-grit sandpaper

Paintable wood-filler putty

Dull red and ivory oil-based exterior spray paints

Dark brown exterior craft paint

Water-based exterior varnish

Basic tool kit (see page 132)

Finished size

Approx. 14 x 11 x 13¾ in. (35.5 x 28 x 35 cm)

interior dimensions

Floor area: 6 x 6 in. (15 x 15 cm)

Cavity depth: 8 in. (20 cm)

Entrance hole to floor: 4 in. (10 cm)

Entrance hole: 2 in. (50 mm) in diameter

cutting list

Front and back panels: 7 x 7½ in. (18 x 19 cm)—cut 2 from straight end of fence board

Side panels: 4¼ x 6 in. (11 x 15 cm)—cut 2 (one side is reserved for the door)

Floor: 6 x 6 in. (15 x 15 cm)—cut 1

Roof: 9½ x 7½ in. (24 x 19 cm)—cut 2

Platform: 13¾ x 7½ in. (35 x 19 cm)— cut 1 from dog-ear end of fence board

1 Cut 2 in. (5 cm) off the top corners of the front and back panels at a 45° angle. Cut a 2-in. (5-cm) entrance hole in the front panel, 4½ in. (11.5 cm) from the bottom and centered on the width. Bevel one short end of each side panel at 45°.

2 Assemble the body of the birdhouse, following steps 2–4 of the Basic Birdhouse on page 9.

3 Glue and nail the roof panels together along one long edge. Glue and nail the roof to the top of the birdhouse, overhanging by 1 in. (2.5 cm) at the back and 1¼ in. (3 cm) at the front.

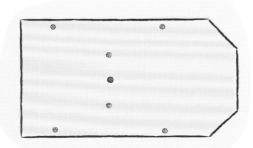

4 Using a ¼-in. (3-mm) bit, drill six pilot holes through the platform and birdhouse floor, then insert 1¼-in. (30-mm) screws. Drill a ⁵⁄₁₆-in. (8-mm) hole through the bottom of the birdhouse to allow for drainage.

5 Measure the distance between the underside of the roof and the porch to determine how tall the pillars need to be, then cut the spindles to length, cutting the top end at a 45° angle. Dry fit the pillars in place to ensure they fit properly, taking care not to cover the screw head for the door. Reserve one of the cut-off tops for the door knob.

6 Measure the distance between the pillars to determine how wide the steps need to be, then cut two steps to the required size from fence board. My steps were 3 x 3¾ in. (7.5 x 9.5 cm). Glue and nail the first step piece against the front wall of the church and the second step piece flat on porch. Cut one more piece for the middle step, approximately half the width of the first two steps, and glue and nail it in place. Remove the pillars and set aside.

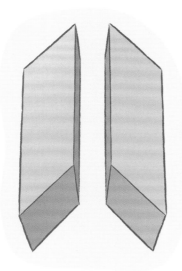

7 From the square 2 x 2-in. (5 x 5-cm) timber spindle, cut two 3¾-in. (9.5-cm) lengths for the steeple, cutting the ends at a 45° angle, as shown. Glue the pieces together. Using a ¹⁄₁₆-in. (1.5-mm) pin bit, drill three pilot holes, then hammer in three nails on each side of the peak to fix the pieces firmly together.

8 Glue the steeple to the center of the roof ridge. Using a ⅛-in. (3-mm) bit, drill a pilot hole through each side of the steeple and into the roof, then countersink 1⅝-in. (40-mm) exterior screws.

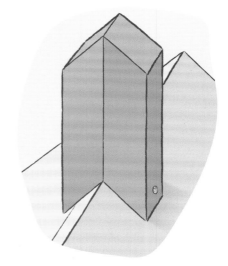

9 Prepare the birdhouse for painting (see step 10 on page 10). Spray with dull red paint and leave to dry. Spray with ivory paint and leave to dry. Lightly sand the birdhouse and steeple, so that the red shows through; do not sand the roof or the steps.

10 Dilute dark brown craft paint (1 part paint to 2 parts water), then paint the roof and porch, wiping off some of paint with a rag if you wish. Varnish.

11 Glue the pillars in place, then nail through the roof into the pillars in three places to secure them firmly. Using a ⅛-in. (3-mm) bit, drill a pilot hole through the porch into the bottom of each pillar, then insert a 1¼-in. (30-mm) screw in each hole.

12 Paint the cut-off spindle top that you reserved for the door knob with ivory paint and leave to dry. Remove the door from the birdhouse and glue the door knob in place. Using a ⅛-in. (3-mm) bit, drill a pilot hole from the back of the door through to the door knob, then insert a 1¼-in. (30-mm) screw.

13 Replace the door. Varnish the exterior of the birdhouse (see page 132).

All hands on deck! With its decorative molding, a rusty bent bolt as the anchor, and wooden sails held by tie wire, this handsome vessel will accommodate a large family of small cavity-nesting birds. I named it after a great friend of mine.

"the nieland" ship **birdhouse**

materials

Two 6 ft x 5½ x ½ in. (180 x 14 x 1.2 cm) dog-ear fence boards (reserve one dog-ear end for top deck)

3 ft (90 cm) decorative chair-rail molding, approx. 2½ in. (6.5 cm) wide, from home improvement store

6-ft (180-cm) length of 1 x1-in. (2.5 x 2.5-cm) wood lumber (timber) for top rails

Waterproof glue

1-in. (25-mm) finish nails or galvanized wire nails

20-in. (50-cm) length of round dowel, ⁵⁄₁₆ in. (8 mm) in diameter

15-in. (38-cm) length of round dowel, ⅜ in. (10 mm) in diameter

10 x 1¼-in. (30-mm) exterior screws

18 x ¾-in. (20-mm) wood screws

Paintable wood-filler putty

80-grit sandpaper

Brown primer, dark red, and tan oil-based exterior spray paints

Dark red, off-white, and dark brown exterior craft paints

Water-based exterior varnish

Two-hole hook, approx. 1½ in. (4 cm) long, with 2 x ½-in. (12-mm) wood screws

34 in. (86 cm) tie wire

Approx. 30 in. (80 cm) black or silver chain link

Rusty bolt or other item for the "anchor"

1-in. (2.5-cm) HS hub connector (from electrical section of home store) (optional)

4 nuts (to use on hub plate) (optional)

1 x 6-in. (2.5 x 15-cm) galvanized nipple (optional)

Two 4-foot (1.2-m) rebars (reinforcing bars), ⁵⁄₁₆ in. (8 mm) in diameter (optional)

Basic tool kit (see page 132) (optional)

Galvanized hollow steel fence post (optional)

finished size

Approx. 20 x 6¾ x 8 in. (50 x 17 x 20 cm)

interior dimensions

Floor area: 8½ x 4¼ in. (21.5 x 11 cm)

Cavity depth: 5½ in. (14 cm)

Entrance hole to floor: 4¼ in. (11 cm)

Entrance holes: 1¼ in. (32 mm) in diameter

cutting list

Front and back panels: 16 x 5½ in. (40.5 x 14 cm)—cut 2

Bottom panel: 10 x 5½ in. (25 x 14 cm) —cut 1

End panel 1: 4 x 4¼ in. (10 x 11 cm)— cut 2

End panel 2: 1¼ x 4¼ in. (3.25 x 11 cm) —cut 2

End panel 3: 1½ x 4¼ in. (4 x 11 cm)— cut 2

Top deck: 20 x 5½ in. (50 x 14 cm)— cut 1 from dog-ear end of fence board

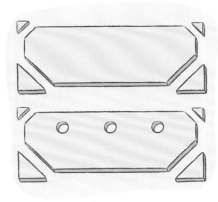

1 Cutting at a 45° angle, cut 1½ in. (4 cm) off the top of the front and back panels and 4 in. (10 cm) off the bottom. In the front panel, cut a 1¼-in. (32-mm) entrance hole 1 in. (2.5 cm) from the top and centered on the width, then cut two more holes, 4½ in. (11 cm) to either side of the center hole.

2 Bevel each short end of the bottom panel at 45°. With the bevels pointing downward, using a ⅛-in. (3-mm) bit, drill pilot holes through the bottom panel into the front and back panels, then drill in 1¼-in. (30-mm) exterior screws. Place one screw 1 in. (2.5 cm) in from each end, with another screw in the center of each side.

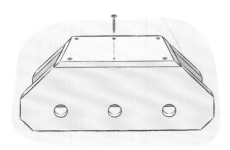

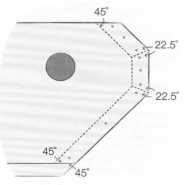

3 Bevel one short end of end panel 1 at 45° and the other short end at 22.5°, with both bevels sloping the same way. Next, bevel both short ends of end panel 2 at 22.5°, with the bevels sloping in opposite directions. Then bevel one short end of end panel 3 at 45° and the other short end at 22.5°, with the bevels sloping in opposite directions. Dry fit the pieces to ensure they're a good fit. Don't worry if you make a wrong cut—you'll have plenty of spare fence board.

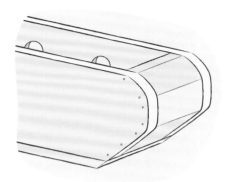

4 Glue and nail the sides only of end panel 1 in place. Repeat with end panels 2 and 3, this time gluing and nailing both the sides and the long edges. Fill any gaps with wood-filler putty and sand smooth: this will give the ends of the ship a rounded shape.

5 Miter the end of the top deck opposite the dog ear at 45° to form a pointed tip. Glue and nail the top deck to the ship, with the pointed end overhanging by 4¾ in. (12 cm); this will be the bow of the ship. The dog-ear end will overhang by 2½ in. (6.5 cm) to form the stern.

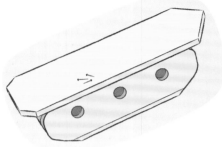

6 Cut a 15⅜-in. (39-cm) length of chair-rail molding and miter each end at 45°, with the miters sloping in opposite directions. Using a ⅛-in. (3-mm) bit, drill seven pilot holes through the molding and into the front panel, just above the bottom panel, in a zig-zag pattern as shown, then drill in ¾-in. (20-mm) wood screws.

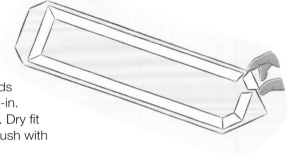

7 Now cut the rails. From 1 x 1-in. (2.5 x 2.5-cm) lumber (timber), cut two 14½-in. (37-cm) lengths for the sides, mitering one end at 45° and the other at 22.5°. For the back rail, cut one 3¼-in. (8.25-cm) length, mitering both ends at 45°. For the front rails, cut one 1¾-in. (4.5-cm) and two 1-in. (2.5-cm) lengths, mitering both ends of each piece at 22.5°. Dry fit the pieces on the top deck, to make sure that all cuts are flush with one another, then glue and nail in place.

8 Cut a 4½-in. (11.5-cm) length of 1 x 1-in. (2.5 x 2.5-cm) lumber (timber) for the center rail to hold the dowels for the sails. Miter cut each short end at 45°. Place in a vice. Using a ¼-in. (6-mm) bit, drill a hole for a ¾-in. (20-mm) wood screw 1 in. (2.5 cm) from each end. Glue, then screw this piece to the center of the top deck. Using a ⁵⁄₁₆-in. (8-mm) bit, countersink the screw nearest the front of the ship to make a hole big enough for a ⁵⁄₁₆-in. (8-mm) dowel. Repeat the process on the right-hand screw, using a ⅜-in. (10-mm) bit.

9 Cut a 13½-in. (34-cm) length of ⁵⁄₁₆-in. (8-mm) dowel and a 15-in. (38-cm) length of ⅜-in. (10-mm) dowel. Pour waterproof glue into each hole and insert the appropriate size of dowel.

10 To make the sails, cut a 5½-in. (14-cm) square from scrap fence board, then cut it in half diagonally to give two triangles. Use one of the off-cuts from the front panel (see step 1) for the third sail. Spray the triangles with dark red oil-based exterior paint and leave to dry.

11 Using a ⁵⁄₁₆-in. (8-mm) bit, drill a hole under each entrance hole, just above the chair-rail molding, and insert a 1¾-in. (4.5-cm) length of ⁵⁄₁₆-in. (8-mm) round dowel into each one for perches.

12 Prepare the birdhouse for painting (see step 10 on page 10), then spray the ship and dowels with brown oil-based primer. Leave to dry. Spray the ship and dowels with tan oil-based paint and leave to dry.

13 Paint the moldings and the perimeter of the deck with red exterior craft paint. Using sandpaper, lightly scuff the edges of the ship and any other areas where you want it to look slightly worn. Drybrush the dowels with off-white exterior craft paint.

14 Dilute brown exterior craft paint (1 part paint to 2 parts water) and brush over the sails and all the red paint on the ship. Dab off excess paint with a rag to create a worn look. Repeat all over the ship. Leave to dry.

15 Varnish the ship, dowels, and sails (see page 132). Leave to dry.

16 Clamp each sail in turn in a vice. Using a 1/16-in. (1.5-mm) bit, drill two holes 1/8 in. (3 mm) apart and 1/2 in. (1 cm) away from the tip of each long edge. Cut six 3-in. (7.5-cm) lengths of tie wire and bend each one in half to form a loop. Push the wire ends through the holes until they protrude by 1/4 in. (6 mm) on the other side.

17 Slide one of the large sails over the taller dowel. Using needle-nose pliers, twist the bottom wire around the dowel 2 1/4 in. (6 cm) from the deck, then crimp tightly in place. Attach the top wire in the same way. Now attach the smaller sail about 1/2 in. (1 cm) above this one, and the other large sail about 2 1/2 in. (6.5 cm) from the top of the shorter dowel.

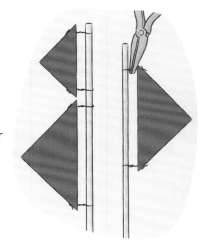

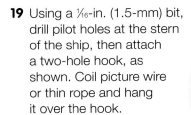

18 Cut two 12-in. (30-cm) lengths of tie wire. Twist them around the dowel "masts" in a cross shape, as shown.

19 Using a 1/16-in. (1.5-mm) bit, drill pilot holes at the stern of the ship, then attach a two-hole hook, as shown. Coil picture wire or thin rope and hang it over the hook.

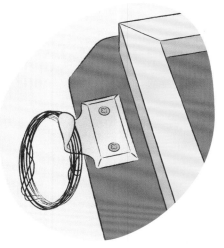

20 Attach a larger link to each end of the 30-in. (80-cm) length of black chain. Pull both ends over the hook, then drape the chain over the front of the ship, around the tall mast, and back to the hook again. Open another large chain link and close it around an old bolt (or whatever you're using for the "anchor"). Using a 1/8-in. (3-mm) bit, drill a small hole in the rail of the ship, slightly off center. Drill in a 1 1/2-in. (4-cm) decorative black screw partway, loop the chain over the top, then tighten the screw so that the anchor dangles over the side of the ship.

21 If desired, attach a hub connector to the base of the birdhouse, then attach a hollow galvanized fence pipe to the base of the feeder, via a length of nipple pipe. Site the birdhouse in your garden, over 4-foot rebars (see page 137).

With its planter boxes filled with colorful flowers, this cute little cottage is quite homely looking. The birdhouses on the left and right are purely decorative, but the one the right lifts up so that you can remove the old nest and clean the main birdhouse interior. The birdhouse can be placed on a shelf or mounted on a post (see page 137).

country cottage
birdhouse

materials

Two 6 ft x 5½ in. x ½ in. (180 x 14 x 1.2 cm) dog-ear fence panels

Waterproof glue

1-in. (25-mm) finish nails or galvanized wire nails

1¼-in. (30-mm) exterior screws for door

1¾-in. (4.5-cm) length of ⁵⁄₁₆-in. (8-mm) round dowel for perch

Two 2-in. (5-cm) squares of chicken wire mesh

2 x 2-in. (5 x 5 cm) wood for chimney

Paintable wood-filler putty

80-grit sandpaper

Brown wood primer paint

Brown oil-based exterior spray paint

Dark walnut, yellow, black, and green exterior craft paints

Small pieces of moss

Metal grommets (eyelets) for flowers

Small ½-in. (12-mm) wood screws

Water-based exterior varnish

Basic tool kit (see page 132)

Finished size

Approx. 14 x 18 x 7¾ in. (35.5 x 46 x 19.5 cm)

Interior dimensions

Floor area: 4¼ x 5½ in. (11 x 14 cm)

Cavity depth: 10 in. (25 cm)

Entrance hole to floor: 8 in. (20 cm)

Entrance hole: 1¼ in. (32 mm) in diameter

cutting list

FOR THE MAIN BIRDHOUSE

Front and back: 12 x 5½ in. (30 x 14 cm) —cut 2

Sides: 9⅛ x 5½ in. (23 x 14 cm)—cut 2 (one side is reserved for the door)

Floor: 4¼ x 5½ in. (11 x 14 cm)—cut 1

Bottom roof: 5 x 5½ in. (12.5 x 14 cm) —cut 2

Top roof: 5¾ x 5½ in. (14.5 x 14 cm)— cut 2

FOR THE RIGHT-HAND BOX

Front and back: 6 x 5½ in. (15 x 14 cm) —cut 2

Side: 2¼ x 4¼ in. (5.5 x 11 cm)—cut 1

Floor: 4¼ x 4¾ in. (11 x 12 cm)—cut 1

Roof panel 1: 1½ x 5½ in. (4 x 14 cm) —cut 1

Roof panel 2: 7½ x 5¼ in. (19 x 14 cm) —cut 1

FOR THE LEFT-HAND BOX

Front and back: 7¾ x 5½ in. (15 x 14 cm)—cut 2

Side: 3¾ x 2¾ in. (9.5 x 7 cm)—cut 1

Floor: 3½ x 2¾ in. (9 x 7 cm)—cut 1

Roof panel 1: 7 x 5½ in. (18 x 14 cm) —cut 1

Roof panel 2: 2½ x 1¼ in. (6.5 x 3 cm) —cut 1

1 Cut the peaks of the front and back panels of the main birdhouse at a 45° angle, reserving the cut-off triangles. Cut a 1¼-in. (32-mm) entrance hole in the front panel, 8½ in. (21.5 cm) from the bottom and centered on the width. Bevel one short side of each side panel at 45°. Assemble the body of the main birdhouse, following steps 2–4 of the Basic Birdhouse on page 9 and positioning the door panel on the right-hand side.

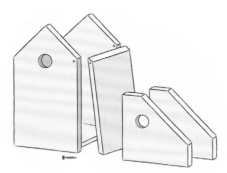

2 Take the front and back panels of the right-hand box. Measure 1½ in. (4 cm) across the top edge, then cut from here to the side at a 45° angle. Cut a 1⅛-in. (28-mm) entrance hole in the front panel, 38½ in. (9 cm) from the bottom and centered on the width.

3 Remove the door from the main birdhouse. Glue and nail the front and back panels of the right-hand box to the front of the main birdhouse door panel, nailing from the back of the door. Glue and nail the side panel in between the front and back panels, then glue and nail the floor panel in place.

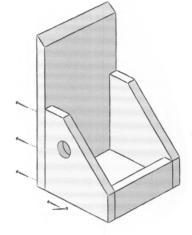

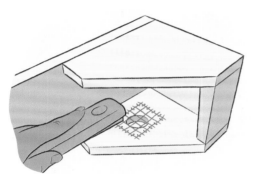

4 Cut a 2-in. (5-cm) square of chicken wire, then staple it to the inside of the hole on the right-hand box, to prevent birds from nesting inside. Re-attach the door to the main birdhouse.

5 Now put the roof on the right-hand box. Bevel both long sides of roof panel 1 at 45°, leaving a ½-in. (12-mm) flat section in the middle. Bevel one short side of roof panel 2 at 45°. Glue and nail the two roof panels together along their beveled edges, then glue and nail the entire roof to the right-hand box, flush with the front and back panels, taking great care not to nail the main birdhouse door shut.

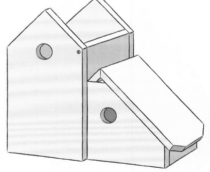

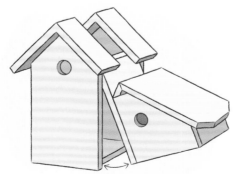

6 Cut the two bottom roof panels of the main birdhouse in half lengthwise, then bevel one short end of each piece at 45°. Glue and nail the panels together in pairs, then glue and nail them to the main birdhouse, following steps 5 and 6 of the Basic Birdhouse on pages 9–10 and making sure that the roof panels do not prevent the door from opening.

7 Bevel one short end of each top roof panel at 45°. Glue and nail them together along the beveled edges, then attach the top roof to the main birdhouse, following step 7 of the Basic Birdhouse on page 10.

8 Take the front panel of the left-hand box. Measure 5¾ in. (14.5 cm) down the left side and cut from here to the top edge at 45°. Make another 45° cut 2 in. (5 cm) long from the top edge to the right-hand edge, reserving this cut-off triangle. Place the front panel on the back panel, draw along the first 45° cut, then draw a line down from the peak to the bottom. Cut along the drawn lines. (The back panel does not have the short 45° cut.)

9 Cut a 1¼-in. (32-mm) hole in the front panel, 3½ in. (9 cm) from the bottom and centered on the width. Staple chicken wire to the inside of the hole, as in step 4. Align the peak of the left-hand box front panel with the edge of the left side of the main birdhouse. Glue and nail in place.

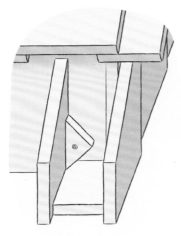

10 Glue and nail the floor panel to the inside of the back panel of the left-hand box. Now, glue and nail the reserved triangle from step 8 to the inside of the back panel. Next, glue and nail the floor to the inside of the front panel. Using a ⅛-in. (3-mm) bit, drill a pilot hole through the triangle into the side of the main birdhouse, then drill in a 1¼-in. (30-mm) screw. Glue and nail the side panel in place.

11 Using a ⁵⁄₁₆-in. (8-mm) bit, drill a hole in the front of the main birdhouse, 1¼ in. (3 cm) below the entrance hole and tap in a dowel perch. Bevel one short end of each roof panel for the left-hand box at 45°. Glue and nail the large roof panel to the top of the left-hand box, overhanging by about 1½ in. (3 cm) at the front and back. Then glue and nail the short roof panel to the large panel along the beveled edge.

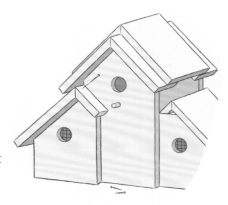

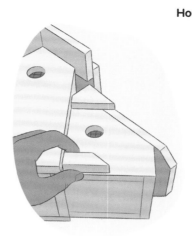

12 Take two of the triangular off-cuts that you reserved from the main birdhouse in step 1. Cut the base off each one, 1¾ in. (4.5 cm) down from the tip. Glue and nail one tip to the front and one to the back of the right-hand box, flush with the peaks. Miter one short end of the door stop at 45°, then glue and nail it to the right-hand box.

13 Cut a 7¾ x 1¼-in. length of fence board and miter one short end at 45°. Glue and nail this piece to the back of the left-hand box, under the roof, for added support.

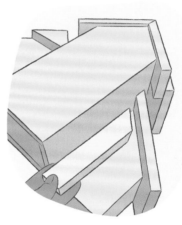

14 Cut across the tip of a 2 x 2-in. (5 x 5-cm) spindle at 45° to give a triangle. Glue and nail this piece to one side of the roof ridge of the main birdhouse to make a chimney.

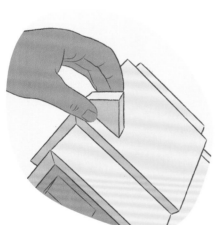

15 Prepare the birdhouse for painting (see step 10 of the Basic Birdhouse on page 10). Spray with brown primer, then leave to dry. Spray with brown oil-based exterior paint and leave to dry. Paint the roof with dark brown exterior craft paint and, while the paint is still wet, drag a rag down the roof to create a worn, aged effect.

16 Cut several small rectangles of scrap fence board for the "planters." Paint each one with dark brown exterior craft paint. Glue and nail them to the front of the birdhouse, following the photo on page 113. Glue small pieces of moss to the top of each planter. Paint the grommets (eyelets) yellow and leave to dry. Insert the grommets above the planters, then paint the screws black so that they look like sunflower heads. Paint on leaf details, using a fine brush and green exterior craft paint.

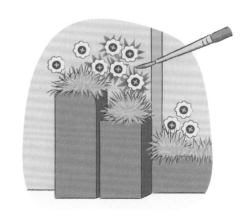

17 Protect the entrance hole by filling it with wadded-up paper, then varnish the whole birdhouse (see page 132).

chapter 5

bird feeders

With so many birdhouses for birds to nest in, you'll want to make a bird feeder to attract a variety of feathered friends to your garden. From a simple pine-cone feeder to a smorgasbord bird feeder, your birds will be in seventh heaven. There's even a nesting basket to help birds with building materials for nests.

This feeder is ever so simple to make, but it will bring you hours of enjoyment as birds flock to it for their favorite food: just throw in a few handfuls of wild bird seed and watch the little guys chow down! The bottom of the feeder has four drainage holes to prevent water from pooling, but do check regularly in case rainwater has caused the seeds to go moldy. To protect the birds from predators, you could mount the feeder on a galvanized steel post (see page 137).

simple bird feeder

materials

One 6 ft x 7½ in. x ½ in. (180 x 19 x 1.2 cm) dog-ear fence panel
Waterproof glue
1-in. (25-mm) finish nails or galvanized wire nails
4 x 1¼-in. (30-mm) exterior screws
16 x 1⅝-in. (40-mm) exterior screws
Paintable wood-filler putty
80-grit sandpaper
One 6 ft x 4 in x 1 in. (180 x 10 x 2.5 cm) lumber (timber)
Brown wood primer paint
Green oil-based exterior spray paint
Dark brown exterior craft paint

5-in. (12.5-cm) length of ¼-in. (6-mm) round dowel for perch
Water-based exterior varnish
Basic tool kit (see page 132)

finished size

13¾ x 9 x 9 in. (35 x 23 x 23 cm)

cutting list

"Birdhouse" façade: 13 x 7½ in. (33 x 19 cm)—cut 1 from dog-ear fence panel

Floor: 7½ x 7½ in. (19 x 19 cm)—cut 1 from dog-ear fence panel

"Birdhouse" roof panel: 8½ x 7½ in. (21.5 x 19 cm)—cut 1 from dog-ear fence panel

Side panels: 8¼ x 4 in. (21 x 10 cm) —cut 2 from lumber (timber)

Front panel: 9⅛ x 4 in. (23 x 10 cm) —cut 1 from lumber (timber)

1 Referring to the Basic Birdhouse on page 8, cut the peak of the birdhouse façade at a 45° angle. Cut a 1½-in. (40-mm) hole, 4 in. (10 cm) down from the peak and centered on the width. Bevel one short end of the birdhouse roof panel at a 45° angle, then cut it in half lengthwise. Paint both sides of the façade and one side of the floor green and leave to dry.

2 Glue and nail the birdhouse façade to the outside back edge of the floor, with the unpainted side of the floor facing up.

3 Using a ⅛-in. (3-mm) bit, drill pilot holes for 1⅝-in. (40-mm) exterior screws through the side panels into the side edges of the floor. Glue, nail, and screw the side panels in place. Attach the front panel to the side panels in the same way.

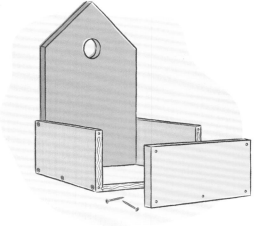

4 Join the two roof pieces together (see step 6 of the Basic Birdhouse on page 10), than attach to the birdhouse façade, flush with the back edge, using 1⅝-in. (40-mm) exterior screws. Prepare the feeder for painting (see step 10 on page 10), then paint the roof top and edges and the outside of the feeder with dark brown exterior craft paint.

European Starling

5 Using a ¼-in. (6-mm) bit, drill a hole 1½ in. (4 cm) below the hole in the façade for the dowel perch (see step 9 on page 10). Gently tap the dowel in place. You may want to put little bit of waterproof glue on the dowel end for extra holding power.

6 To attach the feeder to a fence post via a hub connector, follow the instructions on page 137; use ¼-in. (6-mm) nuts over the hub connector screws to ensure that the points do not stick up into the feeder.

7 Using a ³⁄₁₆-in. (1.5-mm) bit, drill four drainage holes in the bottom of the feeder. Varnish the roof top, the front and back of the façade, and the outside of the feeder box (see page 132).

Birds will bring the whole family to dine at this cafeteria-style feeder, which is equipped with two places to perch, five seed boxes, and a screw in the center to which fruit or a corn cob can be attached. The roof protects the birds from the sun, as well as from the view of any predators flying overhead.

cafeteria
bird feeder

Bewick's Wren

materials

Two 6ft x 7½ in. x ½ in. (180 x 19 x 1.2 cm) dog-ear fence boards

Waterproof glue

1-in. (25-mm) finish nails or galvanized wire nails

30 x 1¼-in. (30-mm) exterior screws

Two 18½-in. (47-cm) lengths of ¼-in. (6-mm) round wood dowel

6ft x 1½ in. x ¾ in. (180 x 4 x 2 cm) pine, cedar, or hard wood

12 x 2½ x ½ in. (30 x 6 x 1.2 cm) pine, cedar, or hard wood

8 x 1⅝-in. (40-mm) exterior screws

1 x 2½-in. (60-mm) exterior screw

80-grit sandpaper

Paintable wood-filler putty

Red exterior craft paint

Water-based exterior varnish

1-in. (2.5-cm) HS hub connector (from electrical section of home store)

1 x 6-in. (2.5 x 15-cm) galvanized nipple

Hollow galvanized fence pipe

Two 4-foot (1.2-m) rebars (reinforcing bars), ⁵⁄₁₆ in. (8 mm) in diameter

Basic tool kit (see page 132)

finished size

Approx. 14½ x 8¼ x 20¾ in. (37 x 21 x 53 cm)

cutting list

Back and base panels: 18 x 7½ in. (46 x 19 cm)—cut 2

Side roof panels: 10 x 7½ in. (25 x 19 cm)—cut 2

Center roof panel: 5¾ x 7½ in. (14.5 x 19 cm)—cut 1

Center roof brace: 2½ x 6¼ in. (6.5 x 16 cm)—cut 1

1 Glue and nail the back panel to the outside back edge of the base panel. Using a ⅛-in. (3-mm) bit, drill four pilot holes along the same edge, then drill in 1¼-in. (30-mm) exterior screws.

2 Cut two right-angle triangles from 7½-in. (19-cm) fence board by cutting across the end of the board, as shown. Cut ¾ in. (2 cm) off one long edge of each triangle.

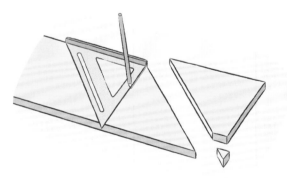

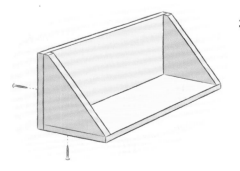

3 Glue and nail the triangular end pieces in place. Using a ⅛-in. (3-mm) bit, drill a pilot hole through the back panel into each end piece, then drill in 1¼-in. (30-mm) exterior screws. Repeat on the base panels.

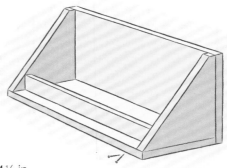

4 Cut one 16⅝ x 1½-in. (42.5 x 4-cm) length of ¾-in. (2-cm) pine or hard wood to create a bracket for the partition dividers. Glue and nail this piece 1¼ in. (3 cm) from the front edge of the box.

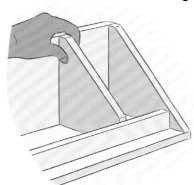

5 Cut two more triangles, as you did for the sides of the box in step 2. Measure the inside of the box to work out how much you need to cut off. Cut to size, then position each triangle 5 in. (12.5 cm) from the inside edge of the box, using a speed square or set square to ensure that they are straight. Glue and nail them in place from the back and the front.

6 Cut two 5 x 3¾-in. (12.5 x 9.5-cm) pieces of scrap fence board; these will form shelves for extra seeds. Bevel one long edge of each piece at 45°. Glue and nail them inside the right- and left-hand sections of the box, placing the 45° bevel-cut edge against the back and making sure that the front is flush with the edges of the triangular pieces.

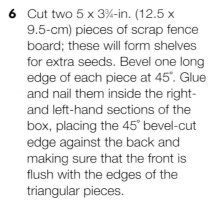

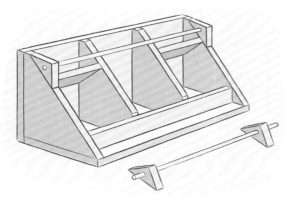

7 From scrap fence board, cut four right-angle triangles, with the short sides measuring 2½ in. (6.5 cm). Drill a ¼-in. (6-mm) hole in the center of each one. Insert an 18½-in. (47-cm) length of ¼-in. (6-mm) round dowel through the holes in two of the triangles, then glue and nail the triangles to the end panels of the feeder, aligning them with the cut-off section of the end panels. Repeat with the remaining two triangles and length of dowel, attaching this perch about 1 in. (2.5 cm) from the bottom.

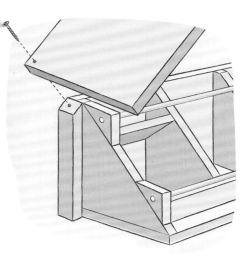

8 Cut two 7½-in. (19-cm) lengths of 1½-in. (4-cm) pine or hard wood as supports for the roof. Bevel one short end of each piece at 45°. These will be used as supports for the roof. Bevel one short side of each side roof panel at 22.5°. Using a ⅛-in. (3-mm) bit, drill pilot holes in the unbeveled ends of each side roof panel, then drill in 1⅝-in. (40-mm) screws through the roof panels and into the supporting pillars.

9 Bevel both short ends of the center roof panel at 22.5°. Dry fit to ensure your cuts are accurate. Place the center roof brace between the roof and the back top edge and nail each end at the bottom. Glue and nail the beveled edges of the center roof panel to the beveled edges of the side roof panels. Nail through the top of the center roof panel to secure it to the roof brace.

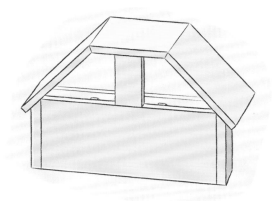

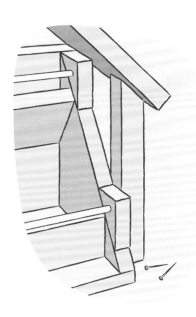

10 Cut two 7⅝ x 1½-in. (19.5 x 4-cm) lengths of ¾-in. (2-cm) pine or hard wood as pillars for the roof. Bevel one short end of each at 45°. Glue and nail the pillars to the sides of the box under the eaves.

11 Using a ⅛-in. (3-mm) bit, drill a pilot hole into the base of the pillars on each each side, then drill in 1¼-in. (30-mm) screws. Drill a pilot hole through the corner of each side roof panel, into the pillars, then drill in 1⅝-in. (40-mm) screws. Drill a pilot hole in the back panel, then drill in a 2½-in. (60-mm) exterior screw—this is used to hold a slice of apple.

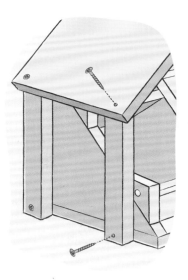

12 Prepare the feeder for painting (see step 10 on page 10). Paint the exterior with red craft paint, leaving the interior, where the birds will perch and feed, free of paint. Varnish the exterior, top and sides (see page 132).

13 Mark the center bottom of the feeder in pencil. Attach a 1-in. (2.5-cm) hub connector over this point, then attach a length of nipple pipe. Mount the feeder on a galvanized steel fence post over steel rebars (see page 137).

Set out a smorgasbord of tasty treats for the birds who visit your garden. Screws run through each side to attach a slice of apple, orange, or corn cob, and there are two trays on the bottom so that you can set out different types of bird seed. Wipe the container clean when it is ready to refill, and check daily to ensure that the food hasn't spoiled. Bring indoors when the weather is harsh, in order to dry, clean, and refill.

House Sparrow

bird feeder buffet

materials

One 6 ft x 5½ in. x ½ in. (180 x 14 x 1.2 cm) cedar fence board

One 6 ft x 3½ in. x ½ in. (180 x 9 x 1.2 cm) cedar fence board

Waterproof glue

1-in. (25-mm) finish nails or galvanized wire nails

14 x 1¼-in. (30-mm) exterior screws

Two 4-in. (10-cm) lengths of ⁵⁄₁₆-in. (8-mm) round dowel for perches

2 x 2½-in. (60-mm) exterior screws

80-grit sandpaper

Paintable wood-filler putty

Bright red exterior craft paint

Old hook or link swivel (available from building supply store) for hanging

1 link swivel from building supply store (optional)

One 24-in. (60-cm) and two 12-in. (30-cm) lengths of heavy black wire

Water-based exterior varnish

Basic tool kit (see page 132)

finished size

Approx. 12½ x 7 x 10½ in. (32 x 19 x 26.5 cm)

cutting list

Birdhouse façade: 11¼ x 5½ in. (28.5 x 14 cm)—cut 1

Roof: 6 x 5½ in. (15 x 14 cm)—cut 2

1 Cut the peak of the façade at a 45° angle and reserve the cut-off triangles. Cut a 1-in. (2.5-cm) hole in the façade, 8 in. (20 cm) from the bottom and centered on the width. Bevel one short end of each roof piece at 45°. Glue and nail the roof pieces together along the beveled edges.

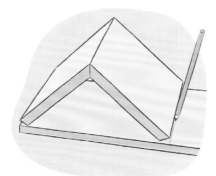

2 Place the assembled roof on the 5½-in.-(14-cm)-wide piece of fence board and mark the end. Cut along your marked line; this gives you dimensions for the buffet floor.

3 Glue and nail the façade to the center of the floor. Glue and nail one of the cut-off triangles to each side of the façade to give it extra stability.

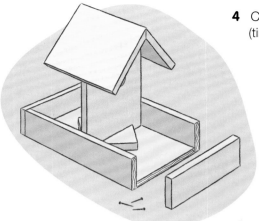

4 Cut two pieces the same length as the floor from 3½-in. (9-cm) lumber (timber). Glue and nail one piece to each side of the floor. Then cut two pieces the same length as the front and back of the floor, including the sides you've just attached. Glue and nail them to the front and back of the floor to complete the feeder.

5 Using a ⅛-in. (3-mm) bit, drill pilot holes at each end and in the center of each side of the feeder, then drill in 1¼-in. (30-mm) exterior screws to ensure the sides are firmly fixed in place.

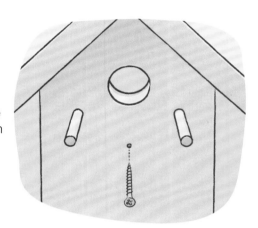

6 Using a ⁵⁄₁₆-in. (8-mm) bit, drill two holes below the hole in the front façade and gently tap in the dowel perches. Using a ⅛-in. (3-mm) bit, drill a pilot hole below the perches, then drill in a 2½-in. (60-mm) exterior screw from which to hang slices of fruit. Drill another pilot hole about 1 in. (25 mm) below this one, but this time drill in the screw from the other side of the panel.

7 Prepare the feeder for painting (see step 10 on page 10), then paint the roof top and the outside of the feeder bright red, leaving the façade and the interior unpainted for the birds' safety.

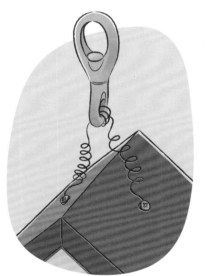

8 Using a ⅛-in. (3-mm) bit, drill a pilot hole in the center of each side of the roof, then drill a 1¼-in. (30-mm) exterior screw partway into each hole. Wrap the end of a 24-in. (60-cm) length of heavy black wire around each screw, then tighten the screw to secure. Wrap the other end of each wire several times around a paintbrush to create a twist, then wrap the twisted wire around a hook or link swivel to make a secure hook for hanging.

9 Using a ⅛-in. (3-mm) bit, drill a hole through each corner of the roof. Twist the center of a 12-in. (30-cm) length of black wire, then feed the ends through each hole from underneath, and twist the ends several times to secure; this forms another perch for the birds.

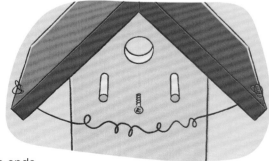

All birds look for materials from which to build and line their nests—and sometimes they take things we would prefer them not to touch. Why not put a selection of nesting materials out there, in the hope that they'll leave your favorite hanging basket alone? Fill this box with yarn, twine, twigs, tall grass, horse hair, dog hair, moss, pine needles—anything that you see the birds stuffing in their beaks and carrying off into the sunset.

nesting material **box**

materials

38-in. (96.5-cm) length of 1 x 1-in. (2.5 x 2.5-cm) square hard wood

3 ft (90 cm) scrap fence material, 5½ in. (14 cm) wide

Waterproof glue

1-in. (2.5-cm) galvanized nails

7 x 5-in. (18 x 12.5-cm) galvanized steel plate from roofing department

4 x 1¼-in. machine bolts with nuts

4 x 1¼-in. (30-mm) exterior screws

80-grit sandpaper

Paintable wood-filler putty

Forest green oil-based exterior spray paint

26 x 9 in. (66 x 23 cm) chicken wire

¼-in. (6-mm) galvanized staples

2 decorative eye snap fastener (from scrapbooking section of craft store)

2 eye hooks

2 small "S" hooks, 1 large "S" hook

Two 12-in. (30-cm) length of ¾-in. (2-cm) chain

Basic tool kit (see page 132)

finished size

Approx. 9 x 5½ x 5 in. (23 x 14 x 12.5 cm)

cutting list

Top and bottom panels: 5½ x 5 in. (14 x 12.5 cm)—cut 2

Roof panel: 7 x 5 in. (18 x 12.5 cm) —cut 1

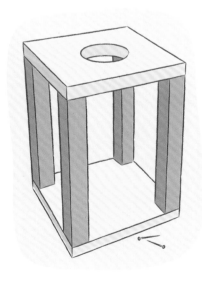

1 Cut a 2-in. (5-cm) hole in the center of the top panel. Cut the square hard wood into four 8-in. (20-cm) lengths, then glue and nail them to the corners of the bottom panel. Glue and nail the top panel to the tops of the 8-in. (20-cm) lengths in the same way to complete the framework of the box.

2 Cut a 2-in. (5-cm) hole in the center of the roof panel. Clamp the galvanized steel plate and the roof panel together. Using a ¹⁄₁₆-in. (1.5-mm) bit, start a hole, then drill a ³⁄₁₆-in. (4-mm) hole in each corner, drilling through both the metal and the wood. Set the steel plate to one side. Insert 1¼-in. (30-mm) bolts in the holes, working from the underside of the roof panel, and secure with nuts.

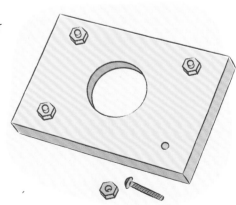

Downy Woodpecker

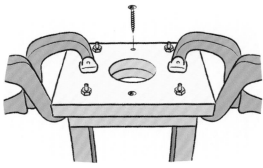

3 Clamp the roof panel over the top panel of the box, aligning the holes. Using a ⅛-in. (3-mm) bit, drill pilot holes through both pieces, then drill in 1¼-in. (30-mm) exterior screws.

4 Prepare the box for painting (see step 10 on page 10), then spray with forest green oil-based exterior paint. Leave to dry.

5 Using wire cutters, cut the chicken wire to fit around the circumference of the box, then staple in place. Clip the ends of the wire as close to the edge of the box as possible, then push any sharp edges into the wood.

6 Using a hammer, gently tap a decorative snap fastener into the center of each side of the box top. Using a ¹⁄₁₆-in. (1.5-mm) pin bit, drill a pilot hole in the center of each snap fastener, then insert an eye hook in each hole. Insert a small S hook into each eye hook, then attach a length of chain to each side, joining them in the center with a large S hook.

7 Unscrew the nuts holding the bolts in place. Place the metal plate over the roof panel, aligning the holes in the corners with those in the wooden roof panel. Screw the nuts back onto the bolts to hold the plate in place. The metal top plate can then be removed so that you can refill the nesting box.

This hand-crafted pine-cone feeder is great for attracting birds to the garden. Easy to make and safe for the birds, it's something all the family can enjoy. Wash the pine cones first, to get out all the dirt and bugs, and leave to dry. The cones will close up, but just leave them in the sun and they will soon open out again. Hang the feeder from a metal hook above a grassy area, where birds will eat any fallen seeds. If you live in an area where there are bears, as I do, bring the feeder inside at night and hang it back up in the morning.

pine-cone bird feeder

materials

7 pine cones, graduating in size, if possible

24-in. (60-cm) length of 2 x 2-in. (5 x 5-cm) pine stick

T-nut

Dark brown oil-based exterior spray or craft paint

10 in. (25 cm) heavy wire

7 x 2½-in. (60-mm) exterior screws

10 in. (25 cm) heavy wire for acorns

3 acorns (optional)

Raffia twine (optional)

1 packet gelatin

¼ cup hot water

¾ cup bird seed

1 Pre-drill holes into the core of the pine cones. It's a good idea to wear leather gloves to protect your fingers.

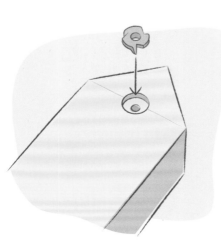

2 Cut one end of the pine stick to a triangular shape. Drill a ⅛-in. (3-mm) hole through for the wire. Countersink a T-nut into the hole (see page 135) to protect the wood from being damaged by the wire. Paint the pine brown.

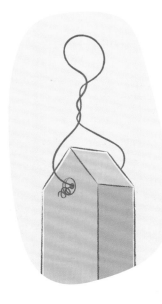

3 Feed a 10-in. (25-cm) length of wire through the hole in the pine stick and twist each end around several times to secure. Twist the wire ½ in. (4 cm) from the top to create a loop for hanging.

4 Starting with the largest pine cone in the center and working outward in order of size in each direction, drill through the back of the stick and attach the cones with 2½-in. (60-mm) exterior screws.

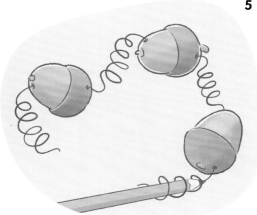

5 Drill a small hole through the base of three acorns. Wrap a 10-in. (25-cm) length of wire several times around a pencil to form "ringlets," thread the acorns onto the wire, then form more "ringlets" at the other end of the wire.

6 Mix the gelatin with ¼ cup of hot water and stir until the gelatin dissolves. Mix in ¾ cup of bird seed and stir well to ensure all the bird seed is coated. Allow to cool slightly. Place the mixture on a cookie sheet (baking tray) covered with foil. Spoon into the pine cones and press firmly. Leave to dry. Hang the feeder from a hook, along with the string of acorns, and tie a raffia bow around the top for decoration.

tools and
materials

Although there are undoubtedly some gizmos and gadgets that will make things easier for you, the birdhouses in this book can all be made with a fairly basic range of woodworking tools and equipment.

basic tool kit

The following tools are what I consider to be the basic requirements for making the birdhouses in this book.

- Miter box
- Hand saw
- Electric chop miter saw
- Power drill
- **Drill bits:** 1/16-, 1/8-, 3/16-, and 5/16-in.
- **Hole saw bits:** 3/8-, 7/16-, 5/8-, 7/8-, 1-, 1 1/8-, 1 1/4-, 1 1/2-, and 2-in.
- Hammer
- Finish nail gun
- Pliers: Needle-nose

- Screwdrivers: Phillips head, straight edge
- Metal tape measure
- Speed square and/or set square
- Vice and clamps
- Old rags/T-shirts
- Paintbrushes ranging in size from 1/4 in. to 1 1/2 in. (6mm to 4 cm)
- Putty knife
- Pencil

wood

CEDAR DOG-EAR FENCE BOARD

I use cedar dog-ear fence board for my birdhouses, for several reasons. First, it's relatively inexpensive. Second, it's actually better for the birds! Fence wood is rough, which means that it's easier for the birds' little claws to grab hold of; it's also untreated, which means that the birds are not exposed to toxic fumes from varnish or paint. And finally, standard fence boards are a good width for the birdhouse panels (5½ and 7½ in./14 and 19 cm)—so you can simply cut across the board without having to take lots of fiddly measurements and markings.

Never use plywood for a birdhouse, as it will warp and fall apart. Smooth wood that is used for building furniture isn't a good idea, either, since it is not rough enough and then you will have to cut grooves in the interior so the birds can use their tiny claws to get out. Press board should definitely not be used for birdhouses—it will disintegrate in bad weather, and it falls apart once your drill screws through it.

ROUND DOWELS FOR PERCHES

Birds need somewhere to alight and perch before they hop down into the birdhouse, and round dowels are just perfect. I usually use dowels that are 5/16 in. (8 mm) in diameter; alternatively, you can use small pieces of driftwood.

1 X 1-IN. (2.5 X 2.5-CM) SQUARE WOOD DOWEL

I use this for the roof ridges in birdhouses that have a Simple Roof (see page 11). You can also use these square wood dowels as door knobs or as a guardrail on the birdhouse front porch.

LUMBER (TIMBER)

Lumber (timber) is used in woodworking for building furniture or as trim around windows, doors, and doorways. It's usually found in the specialty aisles or near the molding department in home improvement stores.

glues, paints, and varnishes

As your birdhouses will be outside and therefore exposed to the elements, it's important that they're as weatherproof as they can be. Be sure to use waterproof glue, so that the pieces are firmly stuck together. Use exterior craft or oil-based spray paints to add color to your birdhouses, and varnish them with exterior varnish. You can also use exterior clear silicone that is waterproof and freeze proof, found in the paint section of a home-improvement store.

N.B. Never paint or varnish the interior of a birdhouse, as this could be very harmful to the birds. Before you paint or varnish, always make sure that the entrance hole is blocked with wadded-up paper or tape, so that no paint will accidentally drift into the interior of the birdhouse.

decorative items

The sky really is the limit when it comes to decorating birdhouses. A lot of the items that I use are either things that I find on walks in the forest, such as pieces of driftwood and pine cones, or things that I recycle from my workshop, such as broken pieces of chain, old bolts, or screws. Home-improvement stores are also a useful source of embellishments—I often add hooks, door knobs, or decorative moldings to my birdhouses. And craft supply stores have loads of pretty things that you can use, from moss and wood shapes to snap fasteners and grommets (eyelets) in the scrapbooking section and vintage-style keys in the jewelry department.

Get into the habit of collecting things like this when you're out and about—you never know when you'll need them! Sometimes when I'm digging in my garden I find rusted faucets or old rusty nails. Save them! They can all be attached somehow, somewhere to the birdhouses.

cutting

In most of the projects in this book, the full width of the dog-ear fence boards is used to create the birdhouse panels, so that cutting is reduced to the minimum. In addition to straight cuts, you also need to know how to make miter cuts (angled cuts, usually at 45°, so that two adjoining pieces will fit together in a tight right angle), and bevel cuts, which means cutting an edge on a slant. You can cut most of the pieces for the birdhouses in this book using a simple miter box and backsaw; the only exceptions are birdhouses that involve 22.5° bevel cuts, for which you will need a compound miter saw. The steps below show how to cut with different tools.

TRADITIONAL WOODEN MITER BOX

Use a traditional wooden miter box and a backsaw for making simple miter cuts. The miter box has slots at 45° (sloping right and sloping left) and 90° into which the backsaw fits, so that you can cut at an accurate angle.

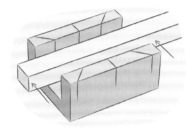

1 Lay the piece you're cutting in the miter box and hold it tight against the back fence.

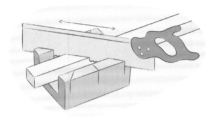

2 Set the backsaw in the appropriate slot of the miter box and make the cut, using slow, smooth strokes, letting the blade do the work. Never force your blade to cut the wood: doing so can result in serious injury.

ADJUSTABLE MITER BOX

There are a number of adjustable miter boxes on the market that allow you to cut miters at any angle from up to 45°.

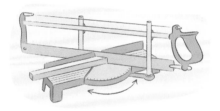

1 Rotate the saw to the desired angle, lock it in place, then make the cut.

COMPOUND-ANGLE POWER MITER SAW

This kind of power saw allows you to make miter cuts and also to bevel the edge of the piece; moreover, you can set both the miter angle and the bevel angle at the same time. As you might expect, this tool is more expensive than the others shown here, but if you do a lot of woodworking, it is well worth buying one for its ease of use and the amount of time it will save you.

Miter cut
To make a miter cut, simply rotate the saw blade to the right or left to the appropriate angle and lock it in place.

Bevel cut
To make a bevel cut, tilt the blade to the appropriate angle and lock it in place; note that some saws only tilt to the left, but dual-bevel models tilt both to the left and to the right.

joining

Joining pieces together is easy when you use the proper tools. I find that having a vice grip on hand helps when gluing and nailing pieces together. Clamps are a must—when your wood decides to warp, you can clamp them together while nailing.

gluing and nailing

I always use waterproof glue and galvanized nails on my birdhouse pieces for extra security. You can screw them together with exterior screws if you wish to make them even more sturdy—just remember to pre-drill pilot holes (see below) for the screws.

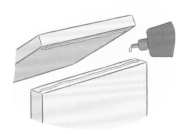

1 Apply a small amount of waterproof glue along the center of the two edges that you are joining together.

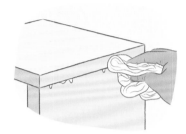

2 Press the edges together, then wipe off any glue that oozes out of the join with an old rag.

3 Using a nail gun, drive 1-in. (25-mm) finish nails through both pieces, making sure your fingers are not anywhere near where the nail could turn and come out, hitting your finger.

countersinking screws

Countersinking screws simply means driving them in so that they sit flush with the surface of the wood. There is a special bit for doing this. The bit makes an indention in the wood above your pilot hole, then the screw head fits snugly, flush with the membrane of the wood. You shouldn't drill the screw head below the membrane, as doing so will cause water to pool and could crack your wood.

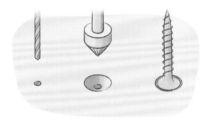

1 Drill a pilot hole for screw (see above). Using a countersink drill bit with a multiple cutting edge, begin making the screw hole. Go down a little way, then remove the drill bit. Place the head of the screw in the hole you've just made to check the size: the hole should be fractionally larger than the screw head.

2 Insert the screw until the head is flush with the surface of the wood. Fill with wood-filler putty, leave to dry, then sand the filler until it is flush with the surface of the wood.

Tip Fill nail and screw holes with glue, and then with paintable wood putty. The glue will help keep the nails from moisture and might help prevent popping from endless expansion and contractions due to changing weather conditions, while the putty with give you a smooth surface for painting.

drilling pilot holes and driving in screws

A pilot hole is a small hole that you drill before driving a screw into a piece of wood. It prevents the screw from splitting the wood and it ensures that the screw will be installed straight, because it will follow the path of the pilot hole. Remember that the bit end gets extremely hot from the friction and can cause severe burns on fingers or hands.

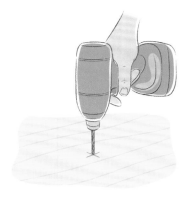

1 Using a pencil, mark on the wood where you want the screw to go. Make a small indentation in the wood using a center punch—a small slender tool with a pointed end. This will help stop the drill bit from slipping when you start the pilot hole. Position the tip of the punch over your pencil mark, then strike the punch gently with a hammer. (For very small screws, you can use a bradawl instead of a center punch.)

2 Insert the appropriate bit into your drill: the bit for a pilot hole should be smaller than the diameter of the screw you're intending to use and, for the projects in this book, a ⅛-in. (3-mm) bit will usually do the job. (Remember that you can always make the pilot hole bigger if you need to.)

3 Place the tip of the bit in the indentation you made in step 2, angling it at the angle you want the screw to follow, then drill the hole to a depth equal to the length of the screw. Back the bit out carefully.

4 Fit your drill with a screwdriver bit. Place the tip of the screw in the pilot hole and drive the screw in, angling it so that it follows the path of the pilot hole.

post-mounted birdhouses

Mounting a birdhouse or feeder on a galvanized steel post is a great way to raise it off the ground and protect the birds from predators such as cats. The method shown here uses items from the electrical and fencing departments of your local home improvement store. HS hub connectors can be found in the electrical section of any home-improvement store, and are generally used for electrical wiring that is on the outside of homes or underground. Rebars are normally used in strengthening concrete.

 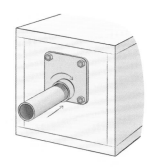 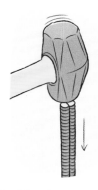 

1 Mark the center of the base of the birdhouse. Place the hub connector hole over your pencil mark. Make a pencil mark through the screw points, then using a ⅛-in. (3-mm) bit, drill pilot holes at the screw points. Screw nuts over the necks of 1¼-in. (30-mm) exterior screws, then drill in the screws to attach the connector to the base of the birdhouse.

2 Screw a 1 x 6-in. (2.5 x 15-cm) nipple pipe into the hub connector, then slide the nipple pipe into a length of hollow galvanized fence pipe.

3 Decide where you are going to position your birdhouse. Using a sledgehammer, pound two 4-foot (1.2-m) rebars/reinforcing bars into the ground to roughly 12–18 in. (30–45 cm), making sure they are secure. Alternatively, you can set the rebars in concrete: dig a 12-in. (30-cm) hole, pour in quick-setting concrete and, when the concrete has partially set, pound in the rebars. Slide the galvanized fence pipe over the rebars.

4 To hold the birdhouse firmly in place, drill pilot holes through the fence pipe from opposite sides and insert bolts, tightening them against the sides of the rebars with a ratchet drill bit (optional).

hanging birdhouses

Hanging birdhouses can be hung from an iron plant hanger, tree limb, or from a hook on your eaves where predators are less likely to reach them. I generally use pipe clamps (clips), which are normally used to clamp a water or electrical pipe to a wall and can be bought from the plumbing department of home-improvement stores, as a base for hanging the birdhouse. You can also use tie wire strung through the roof or through driftwood limbs, which creates a more natural look.

1 Bend a 1-in. (25-mm) two-hole pipe clamp (clip) with pliers to fit on each side of the roof. Mark the center of the apex of the roof. Place the pipe clamp (clip) over the apex at the center point and make a small pencil mark through the center of each hole.

2 Using a $\frac{1}{16}$-in. (1.5-mm) bit, start a hole at each marked point. Screw the pipe clamp (clip) in place with $\frac{3}{4}$-in. (20-mm) exterior wood screws, being careful not to overtighten.

3 You can then either hang the pipe clamp (clip) from a metal hook in your garden, or loop wire through the fastener and hang the birdhouse from the wire.

birdhouse maintenance

With a little care and simple maintenance, your birdhouse should last for years and you will find that birds will return time and time again to nest and bring up their young.

Once the chicks have fledged and the birds have moved out, remove the old nest and clean the inside of the birdhouse so that it's ready for the next season. All the birdhouses in this book have clean-out doors that you can open for easy nest removal. Wear gloves when you do this to ensure you're not infecting yourself with parasites or diseases that may be lingering in the nest. Birds will return to their nest each year, but it's best to remove the nest each season and wash out the interior with soap and water (never use bleach or harsh chemicals) to ensure bacteria doesn't grow, which can cause illness to the new hatchlings. Let the interior of the birdhouse completely dry out, then return it to its original place.

Almost all the birdhouses in this book have been varnished with water-based exterior varnish to protect them from the elements; however, this will not protect them for ever. After you've removed the nest and cleaned properly, revarnish the exterior of the birdhouse, let dry completely for a few days, then return it to its original place. Do this each season a few months before birds start nesting.

If you have extremely harsh weather, bring your birdhouse indoors or set it on a covered porch.

bird safety

We all want to encourage birds to nest in our gardens, but it's absolutely vital to take some basic safety precautions so as not to injure your feathered friends.

❖ Make your birdhouses from untreated, unvarnished timber, as wood preservatives and varnishes are harmful, if not fatal, to birds. I use untreated dog-ear fence board because it's the perfect size for birdhouses for small cavity-nesting birds. The boards are left rough on both sides, so the birds can grab onto it with their tiny little feet and claws for exiting the birdhouse. This is especially important for the young fledglings once they're ready to leave the nest.

❖ Good ventilation and drainage are essential. The roofs of most of these houses are doubled to give plenty of circulation to keep the birds cool. If there is a different type of roof, the ventilation holes are normally drilled on each side of the birdhouse just under the eaves, sloping downward so that water will drip away from the inside of the box. If there is a porch underneath the base of the birdhouse, then simply drill a hole in the center to give proper drainage just in case water finds its way in. It's all about the birds and their comfort. Wouldn't you want to be comfortable in your home?

❖ Many people ask me if the birds will fit through the tiny entrance holes. The answer is yes. Birds that will go into birdboxes generally require a small hole, although there are some exceptions needing larger boxes that are lifted high off the ground. I have never seen a bird turn down a house because the box is 1 in. (2–3 cm) too large or too small. If it fits, it's "home, tweet home!"

❖ When you paint and varnish your birdhouse, make sure that you block up the entrance hole with wadded-up paper or tape, so that no paint or varnish can accidentally stray into the birdhouse interior. Let the paint or varnish dry for a few days before you put the birdhouse out in the garden for the birds to investigate. This will ensure that any fumes or toxins will be well cured and will not distract birds from entering your lovely birdhouse—and the harmful odors will have dissipated by then.

❖ Providing a small dowel perch that protrudes slightly out of and slightly inside the box is a great way to let birds investigate the birdhouse. But remember that the dowel will also give predators something to hang on to when searching out the fledglings. So, be cautious as to how far the dowel is protruding from the outer front part of the box.

❖ Think carefully about where you position your birdhouse. Getting a little sun is good, as long as it's not for a long period of time. Take the time to stand in the place you're planning to put your birdhouse and see how warm the sun is on your face or body. If it's uncomfortable after just a few minutes, think of how it would be if you were inside the bird box.

❖ If you hang your birdhouse, try placing it on a branch that's slightly out from the main trunk, where cats or other predators won't be tempted to dangle from the birdhouse. If you choose to mount it on a tree, place it high enough for the species of bird you're trying to attract. The best (I feel) is on a pipe post where the birdhouse is mounted 6 ft. (1.8 m) off the ground, as the post is slippery, preventing predators from climbing up—but this will need shade from the hot afternoon sun.

❖ Encourage the birds into your garden by providing them with material that they can use to line their nests; see the nesting material box on pages 127–129. You can also leave a ball of yarn, spanish moss, twigs and other stringy objects they will use to build a nest. You can also encourage birds by planting flowers and bushes that provide fruit and seeds.

❖ The projects on pages 118–126 and 130–131 feature a range of imaginative ideas for bird feeders. However, you should never try to attract the birds to your birdhouse by placing food in or on it, as other critters that like to eat bird seed, such as squirrels and chipmunks, will also be attracted. Bird feeders are for the food and birdhouses are for nesting and rearing the youngsters.

birdhouse sizes for different species

Many species of cavity-nesting birds will nest in man-made boxes but, just like humans who are looking for a new home, they have their own preferences and requirements. It's important to know what type(s) of birds you're building the birdhouse for. You'll have greater success attracting the birds you want to your birdhouses if you build them to the proper size.

The entrance hole size probably is the most critical factor when building birdhouses. If it's too small, your chosen bird species may not be able to enter the house. If it's too large, it could allow bigger, more aggressive species to enter. Some species prefer to nest in an open-sided box with the top half of one side of the box removed.

some tips on siting boxes:

❖ Allow the birds a clear flight path to the entrance.
❖ Place the box in a higher, more inaccessible place when there are predators such as cats around; if possible, give the box protection through siting it above a thorny bush.
❖ Ensure that the box is suitably sheltered from rain, so that water will not flood in through the entrance.
❖ Try to have your nest box in place by January or February, as birds will start prospecting for nest-sites early if there is a spell of warm weather (sometimes even the previous fall/autumn!). However, birds will use them at any time of year for roosting, so it is worth putting them up as soon as they are ready.
❖ Keep nestboxes away from bird feeders, as otherwise the occupants will constantly be fending off intruders that come to feed on their doorstep.
❖ The chart below shows some of the most popular cavity-nesting birds of Europe and the United States. Check which ones visit your garden, then design your birdhouse accordingly.

Black-capped Chickadee, Mountain Chickadee, Boreal Chickadee

The Black-capped Chickadee is well known for its mating call of "chick-a-dee-dee-dee, dee-dee"; these birds are a favorite of many who love watching birds in their gardens.

Distribution: All are resident in northern North America: Black-capped in northern half of United States and most of Canada; Mountain in the Rocky Mountains; and Boreal in most of Canada and the extreme northern parts of the United States.
Entrance hole: 1⅛–1½ in. (28–32 mm)
Entrance hole to floor: 5 in. (12.5 cm)
Floor size: 4 x 4 in. (10 x 10 cm)
Box height: 8 in. (20 cm)
Height above ground: 6½–16½ ft. (2–5 m)

Blue Tit, Coal Tit, Marsh Tit, Willow Tit

The Blue Tit is a common visitor to gardens, even in towns and cities, while the other three species are more tied to woodlands and large parks.
Distribution: All species are widespread residents across most of Europe; the range of Coal and Willow Tits extends across northern and central Asia.
Entrance hole: 1 in. (25 mm)

Entrance hole to floor: 5 in. (12.5 cm)
Floor size: 4 x 4 in. (10 x 10 cm)
Box height: 8 in. (20 cm)
Height above ground: 6½–16½ ft. (2–5 m)

Great Tit, Crested Tit

These birds generally prefer to nest in a hole in a tree or wall, but a birdhouse mounted on the side of the house or on a tree trunk will do just fine.

Distribution: Both species are widespread residents in Europe, although in Britain the Crested Tit is restricted to the Caledonian pine forests of Scotland. The range of both species extends into Asia. The Great Tit is a common garden bird in all habitats, even cities.
Entrance hole: 1⅒ in. (28 mm)
Entrance hole to floor: 5 in. (12.5 cm)
Floor size: 4 x 4 in. (10 x 10 cm)
Box height: 8 in. (20 cm)
Height above ground: 6½–16½ ft. (2–5 m)

Barn Swallow, Welcome Swallow, Greater Striped Swallow

Normally swallows are found near barns, nesting inside buildings on ledges and under eaves, and within such buildings they will utilize specially made platforms for nesting.

Distribution: Barn Swallow breeds in temperate regions of North America and Eurasia and winters in Central and South America, south Asia, and Africa. Welcome Swallow breeds in Australia and New Zealand; Greater Striped Swallow breeds in southern Africa.

Floor size: 5 x 5 in. (12.5 x 12.5 cm)
Box height: open-topped, 1½ in. (4 cm) high sides forming a shallow tray
Height above ground: 6½–13 ft (2–4 m), situated against a wall or roof-beam.

Purple Martin

These birds nest in multiples of bird boxes that are specifically designed for the species.

Distribution: East and west North America; they winter in South America.
Entrance hole: 2 in. (50 mm)
Entrance hole to floor: 2 in. (50 mm)
Floor size: 6 x 6 in. (15 x 15 cm)
Box height: 6 in. (15 cm)
Height above ground: 10–17 ft (3–5 m)

Red-breasted Nuthatch, Pygmy Nuthatch, Eurasian Nuthatch

These birds are fun to watch as they climb the sides of trees, scampering upward from side to side finding insects in the bark.

Distribution: Red-breasted is a widespread breeder across northern North America and in the Rockies; winters throughout the United States and southern Canada. Pygmy has a scattered distribution in the western United States. Eurasian is a widespread resident across temperate parts of Europe and Asia.

Entrance hole: 1½ in. (38 mm)
Entrance hole to floor: 6 in. (15 cm)
Floor size: 6 x 6 in. (15 x 15 cm)
Box height: 9 in (230 mm)
Height above ground: 10–17 ft (3–5 m)

Common Starling, Spotless Starling

Starlings can mimic a variety of songbird calls and tend to take over birdhouses occupied by other species. The Common Starling is now considered to be a pest in North America, but it is still favored by many people. The population is in decline in their native Europe.

Distribution: Natural breeding range is across Europe and into Asia; winters south to North Africa; introduced elsewhere around the world including North America, South Africa, Australia, and New Zealand. Common Starling does not breed in Iberia and North Africa, and here it is replaced by the very similar Spotless Starling.

Entrance hole: 2 in. (45 mm)
Entrance hole to floor: 7 in. (18 cm)
Floor size: 7 x 7 in. (18 x 18 cm)
Box height: 10 x 10 in. (25 x 25 cm)
Height above ground: 10–17 ft (3–5 m)

Eastern Bluebird, Western Bluebird, Mountain Bluebird

Everyone in North America wants a bluebird to take a nest in one of their birdhouses—the males of all these species have exceptionally bright blue plumage. These birds will use manmade bird boxes placed in fields on fence posts.

Distribution: Eastern Bluebird is resident in the southern part of eastern North America; is a summer visitor as far north as south-eastern Canada; Western Bluebird is resident in the southern Rockies to Pacific coast, and a summer visitor as far north as British Columbia; Mountain Bluebird is resident the southern Rockies, and a summer migrant as far north as Alaska.

Entrance hole: 1½ in (40 mm)
Entrance hole to floor: 6½ in. (16.5 cm)
Floor size: 5 x 5 in. (13 x 13 cm)
Box height: 9 in. (23 cm)
Height above ground: 6–8ft (2–3 m)

European Robin, Spotted Flycatcher

The Robin is a favorite garden bird in Britain and occurs throughout Europe, while the Spotted Flycatcher is a welcome visitor to large gardens with mature trees.

Distribution: Both species breed across Europe and into Asia. Robin is resident in Western Europe, while Spotted Flycatcher is migratory and winters in tropical Africa.

Entrance hole: No entrance hole—box needs to be open-fronted, with a 2½ in. (6 cm) high panel on the lower half of the front of the box.
Floor size: 6 x 6 in. (15 x 15 cm)
Box height: 9 in (23 cm)
Height above ground: 10–17 ft (3–5 m)

House Sparrow, Eurasian Tree Sparrow, Rock Sparrow

These birds will nest in a manmade bird box placed in the corner of a porch eave, although Tree Sparrows in particular sometimes prefer the box to be situated on a tree.

Distribution: House and Tree Sparrows are widespread residents in much of Eurasia, and they have been introduced in other countries, including the United States. Rock Sparrow is a resident in southern Europe.

Entrance hole: 1⅛ in. (32 mm) for House and Rock Sparrows; 1¹⁄₁₀ in. (28 mm) for Tree Sparrow.
Entrance hole to floor: 6 in. (15 cm)
Floor size: 6 x 6 in. (15 x 15 cm)
Box height: 9 in (23 cm)
Height above ground: 10–17 ft (3–5 m)

Great Spotted Woodpecker, Lesser Spotted Woodpecker, Downy Woodpecker, Hairy Woodpecker

Woodpeckers add a touch of color and excitement to any garden as they clamber about on tree trunks in search of food.

Distribution: Great and Lesser Spotted Woodpeckers are resident in temperate zones across Eurasia, from Britain to the far east of Asia. Downy and Hairy Woodpeckers are resident across North America.
Entrance hole: 2 in. (50 mm) for Great Spotted, 1¾ in. (45 mm) Hairy, 1⅛ in. (32 mm) for Lesser Spotted and Downy.
Entrance hole to floor: 7 in. (18 cm)
Floor size: 7 x 7 in. (18 x 18 cm) for Great Spotted and Hairy; 5 x 5 in. (12.5 x 12.5 cm) for Lesser Spotted and Hairy
Box height: 10 x 10 in. (25 x 25 cm)
Height above ground: 10–17 ft (3–5 m)

Northern Flicker

A boldly spotted and barred woodpecker, this bird is often seen on the ground eating ants.

Distribution: Resident in the United States and mainly a summer visitor to Canada; northern populations winter south in Central America.

Entrance hole: 2½ in. (65 mm)
Entrance hole to floor: 19 in. (50 cm)
Floor size: 7 x 7 in. (18 x 18 cm)
Box height: 24 in. (60 cm)
Height above ground: 10–17 ft (3–5 m)

suppliers

home-improvement stores and building-supply stores
The following are good sources of building supplies, electrical and plumbing equipment, tools, and hardware.

craft stores
The following supply decorative items such as jewelry, fancy keys, sticks, driftwood, moss, buttons, shells, and so on.

US

ACE HARDWARE
www.acehardware.com

THE HOME DEPOT
www.homedepot.com

LOWES
www.lowes.com

UK

B&Q
www.diy.com

HOMEBASE
www.homebase.co.uk

WICKES
www.wickes.co.uk

US

CREATE FOR LESS
www.createforless.com

MICHAELS
www.michaels.com

SAVE ON CRAFTS
www.save-on-crafts.com

UK

CRAFT SUPERSTORE
www.craftsuperstore.co.uk

HOBBYCRAFT
www.hobbycraft.co.uk

HOMECRAFTS DIRECT
www.homecrafts.co.uk

index

acknowledgments

I could never have started my birdhouse business or written this book without the support of many people in my life.

First and foremost, I want to tell my husband Guido how much I love him and to thank him for supporting me every step of the way, for cooking dinner when I was unable or too busy to stop, and for taking on all the work that I should have been doing. Without your support, I could have never accomplished all my journeys.

Thank you to my best friend Ginny for taking my calls in the middle of the night; for teaching me how to use Microsoft Word, which I've had for years and didn't use to its full potential; for helping me edit, staying up late, bringing the wine and for your confidence in my work. We will always be best friends. I love you, Missy!

Thank you to my buddy, best friend Mark, for helping me figure it all out at the beginning; for the all-day brain-storming sessions on your technical computer; and for being there when you were too busy but still took the time to listen.

Niki, if it wasn't for you and your technical Internet support and putting up with all my constant emails and cries for help, I would not what I am today. What is the definition of genius? Niki, that's what!

Jodean, if it wasn't for you giving me the opportunity to place my creations in your gift shop, I would not be here writing this. Thank you for all you've done for me. I am blessed with special friends.

Thank you to CICO Books for contacting me and trusting in me to do this book project. Thank you for putting up with all my emails of questions. All of you have been so kind and patient. This is an opportunity of a lifetime and I appreciate everything that has been done to create my book and get it on its way.

Thank you to Sarah for being so patient in deciphering all my instructions. It was a pleasure working with you, although through email, it seemed like I've known you for years and you made me feel so comfortable.

To Cindy, Clare, and Carmel—thank you for all you've done in getting the ball rolling. It was a pleasure working with you; without all of you, none of this would have been a reality. Thank you, Steve, for the beautiful illustrations you've created. The book wouldn't be complete without all your hard work. Thanks to photographer Caroline Arber and stylist Sophie Martell for such magnificent photos of my creations. The birdhouses look stunning against the green foliage, bringing them to life.

Thank you to anyone and everyone that I have forgotten or didn't mention. You all rock in supporting my decision to do this book project and I love you all. Thank you for understanding why I disappeared and never called or stopped by. It will all be worth it in the end.

We dream, therefore we follow our dreams. Think positive and make the best of each day. Never stop learning and discovering your potential—you may surprise yourself in what you can learn and do.